IN THE SHADOW
OF A BADGE

A SPIRITUAL MEMOIR

IN THE SHADOW OF A BADGE

A SPIRITUAL MEMOIR

LILLIE LEONARDI

Printed in the United States of America.

ISBN: 978-1-59571-739-9

Library of Congress Control Number: 2011940382

Archangel's Heart illustration: Sam Corey

Designed and published by:

Word Association Publishers
205 Fifth Avenue
Tarentum, Pennsylvania 15084

www.wordassociation.com
1.800.827.7903

DEDICATION

To God:

For illuminating my life's journey and purpose.

To the loves of my life:

Vanessa, Jada, Bella, Kayla and Nicky…you are my heart's content.

To my Muses:

Michael the Archangel and the Angels…you inspired me to write.

To my Mother:

Mom… you gave me the courage to move forward.

To my brother:

Sam…you encouraged me to pursue my dreams.

To my dearest friends:

Bill, Connie, Judy, Lisa, Michele, Pierina, Stacy and Terri …you supported my dream.

To all of the Agency Representatives who responded to the Flight 93 crash site:

For serving in the best interest of your fellow man.

To Bill Hobgood, Denise Harvill and the United Airlines Humanitarian Response Team:

For the compassion you showed the victims and families of Flight 93.

And…

Most especially to Cally…for all of your tireless efforts in making this book possible.

TABLE OF CONTENTS

Foreword 9

Preface 11

Chapter 1: A Day of Infamy: September 11, 2001 15

Chapter 2: The Race Toward Destruction 26

Chapter 3: A Field of Angels: Shanksville 31

Chapter 4: The First Few Days at the Crash Site 43

Chapter 5: The United Airlines Team 49

Chapter 6: A Mother's Agony 58

Chapter 7: The Days at Seven Springs 62

Chapter 8: The Memorial Services 68

Chapter 9: The Return Home 73

Chapter 10: The Reckoning Between Mind and Spirit 78

Chapter 11: First Confession 82

Chapter 12: A Reflection of Mary Magdalen 87

Chapter 13: A Traumatic Injury 90

Chapter 14: The Flashbacks: A Return to the Scene 98

Chapter 15: A Spiritual Surrender 102

Chapter 16: The Dark Night of the Soul 104

Chapter 17: The FBI Meets FEMA 109

Chapter 18: A Voice in the Wilderness 113

Chapter 19: Superwoman Has Left The Room 117

Chapter 20: A Secret Revealed 122

Chapter 21: A Lily in Bloom 130

Chapter 22: Reconciliation of My Mind and Soul 135

Chapter 23: Weeding Through 139

Chapter 24: The Southwest Trail 142

Chapter 25: Life's Purpose 146

Chapter 26: A Tale of Two Muses 154

Chapter 27: A Christmas Shawl 159

Chapter 28: The Return of an Old Pattern 168

Chapter 29: Looking for a Piece of Myself 172

Chapter 30: EMDR Therapy 177

Chapter 31: A Symbol of Resurrections 182

Epilogue 185

Author's Closing Note 186

About the Author 187

FOREWORD

Dear Dad,

I just wanted to take a moment and extend my deepest gratitude to you for all you did for me. You were an excellent Father and friend. I am extremely grateful to you for all of the gifts which you gave to each of us, your children and your family. You provided us with a wonderful mentor and taught us about love, life, integrity and values. You inspired us to become the best that we could be. You often told us we your children were "your gold and silver in this life." I hope that you are looking down and seeing us shine in your light. You planted the seeds and now you are watching us grow. We have grown into your mirrored image. I hope you relish all of our successes. For our successes are your legacy.

Also, I wanted to thank you for taking the time to teach me about God. You taught of God's endless love and forgiveness for His children. You preached that God continued to love us even in the times in our lives when we faltered and strayed from the path which He had designed for us. You read us the stories of the Bible and provided us some insight into the wonders of God's mercy. You allowed us the opportunity to dream and have hope for a better life. As a result of your teachings, on a fateful day ten years ago, I reached into the vast recesses of my soul and cried out to God for His help. Oh, and did He respond. God sent the world the gift of His angels. The angels which I read about as a child and often believed that I saw. I did see them that day in all of their brilliance and light. On September 11, 2001, God extended His hand and surrounded the world with his infinite love and guardianship. God sent His angels to protect those of us responding to the site and to gently carry the victims of Flight 93 to His Heavenly home. He provided passage and comfort to those who had sacrificed their lives in the name of honor. I was privileged to have observed the magnitude of His mercy and love.

I now release the story of Flight 93 and the field of angels in honor of my two Fathers. In the worst moments of my life, I felt both the presence of my heavenly and earthly Father's love, kindness and patience. As you look down from Heaven Dad, I hope you are proud. I hope that you smile and look around and say, "Look at my daughter." For I look around on a continuous basis and say, "Look at all my Father has bestowed upon me." I have been truly blessed.

Rest easy Daddy, I'll see you when I see you…

PREFACE

WHEN I LOOK AT PEOPLE, I SEE THEIR SOUL. I witness the internal source of their being, not the external truth of the person. I see the purity which is derived from their spirit buried within the caverns of their body and connected to their mind.

This was always a problem for me because I wanted to see the enlightened soul of one and all. Yet this insight was in direct conflict with the career I had chosen. As a law enforcement professional, I had to learn to lead with my mind, not my heart. To trust my primal instincts, not my emotional responses. If I was to survive in this new world of policing, I needed to quickly become less trusting of my fellow human beings and more calculating as I learned to immediately evaluate the person in front of me.

Living in these two different worlds, I spent all too much time not acknowledging my true self. It was a lifestyle that nearly shattered my life and left my doctors who treated me for Post Traumatic Stress Disorder wondering how my mind had survived. And it almost cost the loss of the most precious parts of me, that of my heart and soul.

This insight, which represents the dichotomy of my person, also explains my two-dimensional writing style. The first is formatted from the linear side of my brain and authored in a formal and direct manner similar to the style I was required to write as part of documenting many a police report. This style is how I perceived my world of policing and its visual context and effects. At times, these pages will reflect my law enforcement background as it takes hold in a very clear and precise way. It is the first voice of my character and the one you will hear as you read the chapters of this book.

The second writing style is poetic in its context. I am told it is "flowery" in its design. It mirrors that of my heart and soul. It delivers to the reader a glimpse of the inner sanctum which I hold closest and protect. As I write in this second mode, I can hear it, feel it and see it as I type. The words have a life of their own and pass easily from pen to paper. It is as if some being has taken hold of my inner creativity and has set it free. My Muses come to life and my spirit soars to a higher level, at the time I am writing.

As I wrote this book, it became exceedingly clear as to why my mind was so convoluted these last years. I was living in this world with one foot firmly planted on the Earth, and the other soaring in an ethereal domain. I was living in two separate and distinct worlds which, over time, became so entwined it was virtually impossible for my mind to fully function under the pressure of it all.

The authoring of these chapters has helped to bring my life to a pivotal point of healing and evolution. By living in two worlds, I almost drove myself to destruction. The healing has prompted a better understanding of myself and the inner workings of my heart, my mind and my soul. It has made me keenly aware there is no longer a need to live in varying worlds, but to intertwine the two and live as one.

The following chapters provide the tale of 9/11 that caused my two worlds to collide and set the stage for the transformation of my soul. The story details aspects of my life as I lived it. Shadowed by a badge. Telling it has enabled me to realize there is no longer a need to stay hidden behind that metal shield. It is time for me to step out and allow the illumination of my soul to shine forth again and become the predominant part of my being.

CHAPTER 1

A DAY OF INFAMY:
SEPTEMBER 11, 2001

SEPTEMBER 11, 2001, BEGAN AS ANY ORDINARY late summer day in Western Pennsylvania. The weather held promise of being clear, bright and hot. It was the time of the year that I looked forward to with the heat of the day, the cool crisp nights and the changing color of the leaves dangling from the trees. The delightful weather and the seasonal changes always seemed to lift my mood. The early days of September were also a busy time with work too. The month brought the beginning of a new school year and, as the Community Outreach Specialist for the Pittsburgh Division of the Federal Bureau of Investigation (FBI), much of my day would focus on prevention and intervention programming in the numerous school districts within my jurisdiction.

This particular day had already been filled with preparations for work and I was soon ready to leave. Being a creature of habit, I had an early morning routine which included drafting notes for daily meetings and other activities related to that specific day. I had already completed documenting the initial information needed to compose the daily reports. This information was used to compile the monthly and a portion of the bi-annual reports for review by FBI management. The bi-annual report provided an overall picture of all projects which the Pittsburgh Field Office engaged in as part of the extensive Community Outreach Program (COP).

The Pittsburgh Field Office COP had received a great deal of recognition, both for the initiatives developed and the external partnerships established. The outside partnerships were vast and included representation from federal, state and local government, law enforcement agencies, child protective services, community and youth-based groups, non-profit organizations, school districts and elected officials.

As coordinator and manager of the program, I was very proud of the collaboration and accomplishments of COP's external partners—each were very dedicated to their "call to service." All worked in tandem to address, intervene, respond and resolve the problematic issues in the cities and schools. More specifically, we all united in a collective cluster to prevent and decrease the violence and crime plaguing our communities. Regardless of the societal issue, the collaborative team worked to help eliminate issues such as drug and alcohol abuse, gang violence, street crime and other problems which arose.

Addressing the needs of children was the primary focus of COP's many initiatives and was always the work that gave me greatest pleasure. Through the prevention and intervention programs which were developed and conducted in partnership with so many amazing people, the youth received much needed guidance. Additionally, many of the agency representatives were involved in mentoring too. For many years, each of us had worked tirelessly in the "best interest" of our children.

As I went outside that morning, the warmth of a brilliant sun greeted me. Standing on the front porch, draped in sunlight, the brilliant rays of the sun flooded through me and lifted my spirit. I stood there for a moment or two just breathing in the fresh air and admiring the beauty of the day.

I walked the short distance from the porch to my Bureau-owned vehicle (known in my circle of colleagues as the "Bucar") and attempted to start it. But after numerous attempts the engine would not turn over. Having very limited knowledge about mechanics, it appeared to me that the battery was dead. At that point, I became completely frustrated because I knew I would now be late for my first meetings of the day. Muttering a few curse words, I got out of the car, called the Field Office to alert my supervisor of the problem and contacted the Division's on-duty mechanic. The mechanic informed me he would be out to tow the vehicle into the garage in about an hour's time.

I returned inside my home and began to make several telephone calls to cancel my morning appointments. With each conversation, I became increasingly more agitated at the prospects of my tardiness and my need to reschedule several meetings. The rescheduling only compounded my feeling of frustration. As I awaited the arrival of the mechanic, I turned on ABC's Good Morning America to get caught up on the early news of the day. I gazed at the television screen only half watching, seeing what appeared to be footage of a plane striking a tall building in New York City. I remember wondering if this was raw footage from some upcoming television show or one of those dramatic trailers used to heighten the interest of a future moviegoer. I also recall hearing Diane Sawyer say that the newsroom had just received confirmation that the plane had indeed struck one of the Twin Towers located in downtown Manhattan.

As the news of the plane and a live shot of the Tower appeared on the screen, the story of 9-11 began to unfold. Instinctively, my background in policing kicked in. I knew the incident was not an accident, but an intentional act. And I wondered, who had perpetrated such a heinous crime? All of my years of police training did not prepare me for the events that the world would now witness. I watched as the camera stayed fixed on the first Tower. I was terrified at the sight of the large gaping hole in the upper floors of the building. Glass and steel were exploding and sending remnants of the structure crashing to the pavement below. The Tower became a burning inferno with its black smoke and orange flames in dramatic contrast to the quiet morning sky. It looked like some ancient volcano on the verge of an eruption, ready to wreak havoc on the inhabitants and streets of New York City.

I was transfixed on the first Tower. And just as my mind began to settle, the second plane flew toward Tower Two. It struck the building with such blunt force that the outcome for human survival seemed impossible. Soon, each of the subsequent events flashing on the television screen appeared more horrific than the last. Inside the towering infernos, victims began jumping from the windows. These first victims of the Towers were making the choice to risk the fall versus the flames they now faced. My heart ached for each of them and for the choice they felt forced to make. My thoughts strayed to their families. How would they feel if they recognized a loved one plunging toward their death? How would they ever be able to erase from their mind that last agonizing glimpse?

The fire now appeared to have a life force of its own. The next scenes were that of the emergency response vehicles racing to the Towers. The newsreels showed hundreds of vehicles swiftly parking in front of the Towers. Once parked, the emergency response personnel rushed to the buildings' entrances. As these uniformed men and women ran inside the Towers and disappeared from view, I wondered if they did so knowing full well that they may not survive. In their attempt to save the lives of others, they may indeed become the tertiary victims of this horrific event.

My mind flashed back to the moments in my own career as a police officer. How often had I performed some task which required me to aid or resolve a situation? Many events and memories of my days wearing blue filtered through my mind: the thoughts of my responses to each incident, the mindset which would take hold of my being, and the training I received would instantly kick into gear as I heard a familiar mechanism click in my head. It all surfaced as I watched the Towers ablaze.

When I speak of a "mechanism," it is hard to describe its meaning. Because it is not a sensation or a feeling, but a mechanical occurrence which rapidly prompts a spontaneous reaction from me. Typically, it also occurs among others who wear the blue. For me, it was a learned confidence that came from rote memory development after extensive practice during my training at the Academy and first years as a police officer.

In retrospect, I believe, I always had this mechanical ability. So, not surprisingly, it became a part of my personality. Even as a child, if something bad happened or one of my siblings was injured, I was ready and willing to aid them. It didn't matter about the amount of blood or if someone was crying in pain, I looked past my fear and responded as needed. I recall that in my youth, my younger siblings would feel so much better if I was with them after they were hurt. On all too many an occasion, I would hold one of them in my arms as Mom drove the car to the hospital. It seemed to quiet their fear. Even now when something bad happens, my daughter often uses a saying, "If the world is falling apart, you want Mom to help. She always knows what to do."

Occasionally, throughout my later days as a police officer, my daughter would call me, "Robocop." It was her definition of the very mechanism which I speak of. My daughter, now in her thirties, has told me that a transformation often took place whenever I wore my uniform. Something would take hold of me and erase any essence of humanity. I was no longer her Mother, but some robotic persona. She claimed my demeanor would change, and I even walked and talked different. There were times when my daughter would say to me, "Hey, Robocop, my Mom is missing and I want to file a report. When you find her, will you ask her to come home because I miss her?"

At first, I took great offense to my daughter's words because they sounded so harsh and disrespectful, and unnerved some part of me. But as time moved on, I realized she was speaking the truth all too clearly. In that particular time in my life, I was not aware of the change in my personality. And I was not capable of accepting it either. But now, as I reflect upon these past years in my profession, I realize that she was right. I did possess an alter ego and an identity which was separate and distinct from my true essence.

My femininity seemed to dissipate each and every time I buttoned the starched shirt of my police uniform and placed that badge over my heart. The badge became more of a symbol for the robotic person to come to life than that of a shield to protect my heart. But, it wasn't used to protect me in the way in which I had hoped it would. The badge became a symbol for hiding my true feelings and burying them underneath in some deep cavern. It was there to shield me from the pain and the memories of all of the negative things I would see in the prevailing years to come.

As my heart became shielded from any emotional responses, the mechanism replaced them. And as I would respond to a call for service, I would hear the tiny clicking sound ringing in my ear each and every time. With the first click, I focused my attention on the situation and all of the details would filter through my mind. With the second click, my mind would center on the action necessary and the tunnel vision would take hold. With the third click, my mind determined the action necessary. And, with the fourth and final click, my mind and body became ready to spring into action. As the mechanism switched on, so did the transfer of my behavior. It was not necessary for me to shed my glasses like Clark Kent as he switched from the mild-mannered reporter to his second persona, that of Superman. No, it took little conscious effort on my part to become "Robocop" and to fine tune my mind in preparedness to respond and to survive. The desire became primal and my instinct heightened in order to succeed in protecting my life and any others as necessary.

As my mind refocused on the events of this September day, and an incident of such magnitude, I was saddened for the responding officers who would be required to "stir up" the great energy and courage needed. I prayed for their well-being and for their guardian angels to protect and guide them as they moved through the burning buildings in search of survivors and victims alike.

It was just then that Diane Sawyer announced a third plane had struck the Pentagon in Washington, D.C. and that the City was being evacuated. She indicated that there was a suspicion of a fourth plane involved in this plot, but its whereabouts and destination were yet unknown. But minutes thereafter, the news of a plane crashing in the remote field of a landfill located in Western Pennsylvania echoed across the television screen.

Each of these incidents followed the other, as if placed in a systematic order of a staged event or movie. The cumulative impact would soon be heard and felt around the world. And a new generation of young Americans would be identified by these heinous events. It would be their legacy to withstand. The events of 9-11 would live in infamy for this generation, just as the Vietnam War had been identified with mine and World War II and Pearl Harbor with that of my parents.

As I listened to the news, I wondered what was next. As these thoughts crossed my mind, I turned back to the television set and watched in disbelief as the Towers began to crumble under the heat of the flames. I heard the sound of the once mighty Towers as they screamed in a thunderous roar at the strength of the fire within. As Tower One fell, I observed and felt the horror of all who were present. The look of terror and disbelief were present in the many faces of the victims running away from the scene. Those of us, who watched and witnessed the carnage via our television screens, instinctively felt the same deep set of emotions in the recesses of our souls. I felt immobilized and helpless as I watched New York City and its inhabitants become paralyzed with fear. Thousands of bystanders were unable to help their fellow human beings. People were panicking and running to save their lives as the remnants of the Towers came raining down upon them and swept across the sea of people, streets and sidewalks of the City.

The vision of the crumbling Towers with the smoke and white powder moving in every direction resembled a great tsunami wave which was about to swallow all in its path. In my mind's eye, the faces of the innumerable persons affected by the morning's events—the news media, the emergency responders, the random victims and even that of President Bush as he sat in contemplation at an elementary school in Florida—appeared in a kaleidoscopic manner.

A deep sense of pain began to churn inside of me as I watched the television. And like most others viewing, I cried for those who had been lost and injured. My heart wept, my tears fell and I knelt upon the floor. My prayers began to flow and I heard my voice softly whisper to God for His aid. The aftermath of bewilderment began to take hold as I sat glued to the television and wondered, what next?

My first impulse was one of parental concern. Was my daughter, who worked for the United States Attorney's Office, safe? Was my granddaughter, who was in her first days of kindergarten, being protected? Where was the rest of my family and were they alright? How could I protect them? Would there be any more attacks? How could I help? I called my daughter on the telephone. She was alright but afraid. She began to cry and asked questions as to what should she do. I told her that I loved her and she should take every precaution for her safety. She should follow the direction of the building's Security Officer and find a safe passage to her home. As she asked more questions, my mind reverted to an instantaneous need to care for her. Although I had just seen her earlier that morning, my heart ached to put my arms around her and soothe away her fear. As my mind raced between my need to reassure her and my intent to get moving, I reiterated my love for her. I told her to be careful and to take great care of herself and my granddaughter. I told her not to worry because I fully trusted that God would see all of us through this crisis. And I told her if for some reason I didn't get to see her again, she should remember I dearly loved both her and the little one. I ended the conversation by saying, "Even when I'm gone you'll know that I'm near each time the wind blows through your hair. When the wind moves, imagine my hand is resting on your head and listen as my voice whispers the comforting words you need to hear. I'll never be too far away."

As I spoke these words, I realized that my paternal Grandmother had told me a similar story about herself and our eternal connection of one to the other. My grandmother had often explained that even after her death she would always been near. She would appear in the form of a dove. Each and every time I saw a dove, it should remind me that she was present in my life. Now, in my moment of need, I wished for the appearance of a dove and the presence of my grandmother too. I dearly needed a sign to indicate some form of comfort was near.

As I hung up the phone with my daughter, I wondered how many other mothers would connect with their children in the moments following this event. How many others would not be able to reach their children or, tragically, never hear the voice of their own dear child again? I remember saying a prayer and thanking God for the opportunity to have been able to hear my daughter's voice. I prayed for her protection, for that of my grandchild and for the rest of my family. I prayed for those who were injured or killed and for strength to serve my community.

My mind began to move from that of mother, grandmother, daughter and sister to that of a law enforcement officer. I immediately contacted the Pittsburgh Division's communication desk and was advised to stand by because the office was awaiting orders from FBI Headquarters. I then contacted a Division Administrator and immediately volunteered my services to respond to Shanksville or any of the other sites where help might be needed. I was told to report to the office because staff members were needed to respond to the Shanksville site to set up a mobile command and help arrange the necessary ancillary services to prepare for an all agency response.

CHAPTER 2

THE RACE TOWARD DESTRUCTION

I RAN FROM MY HOME AND JUMPED into my personal vehicle. I felt like a television super hero leaping into a car and preparing to respond to some crime perpetrated by an unknown villain. I raced through traffic to the field office. I was oblivious to the movement of traffic or the speed of my car. As my foot pressed harder on the gas pedal, my tunnel vision began to take hold. My mind became transfixed by the mission ahead. I needed to get to the FBI Office as swiftly as possible.

In my car, I once again assumed the role I had played as a patrol officer some seventeen years prior. As my thoughts raced, I became mesmerized in the recalling of my first high-speed chase. I remembered the sensation of my breathing and that of the adrenalin surging through my body. The fear erupting inside me and feeding the raw adrenalin as it coursed through my veins. The force of nature that triggered these emotions, creating a singular tunnel vision to stop the threat ahead. It was a voice that would quietly speak to me and repeatedly echo to my inner consciousness the words, "drive, drive, drive." It was the amygdala of my brain ordering and preparing me for battle.

My tunnel vision remained on the image of the chase and my maneuvering of each turn. My immediate focus, however, stayed on the road ahead and the twenty odd miles yet to travel. I felt no emotion. I felt only the clicking of the trained mechanism in my head. The training mechanism which was all too familiar to me from my past days as a cop.

With each click, I felt the evolution of a restrained calculated calm beginning to set in. It was a calming sensation which was drilled into me, and each of my fellow cadets, day after day in the early days at the Police Academy. This known feeling meant only one thing: my entire being was preparing for the unknown battle ahead. The training took hold and the law enforcement officer emerged. My true self quickly slipped away to the second personality known all too well to my family. The once loving daughter, mother, granddaughter, sister and friend gave way to the seasoned veteran of the street. I had heard the "call of the wild" inside my soul and the warrior in me had responded. The transformation to the robotic trance had begun and survival became the paramount issue at hand. The old familiar robotic stance had gained control of me and would stay intact for the next 13 days.

When I arrived at the office, there were people scurrying in every direction. My colleagues were geared up and readying the command post for action. The command post would become the epicenter of all activity. It would be the location in which all major decisions were made. It would be the "hub" where the field office administrators would receive all the orders generated from FBI higher echelon in Washington, D.C. The command post would be operated on a 24-7 schedule with three shifts of personnel working around the clock. Since, I had already called ahead and spoke to an Administrator, I was immediately requested to assist two other employees in transporting mobile command to the Shanksville crash site. I agreed to accompany the two other employees and work in any capacity needed.

As I left the building, I became cognizant of the fact that I was about to enter a domain I hoped I would never have lived to see. At that precise moment, I questioned my ability to assume the role necessary to accomplish the multitude of tasks which would need to be addressed. In the few minutes it took to drive to the off-site garage, I stilled my mind and began to hear the familiar clicking echoing inside my head once again. It didn't take long to arrive at the off-site garage where the mobile command unit was parked and all too soon I pulled into the ramp of the metal structured building. I spent the next minutes in haste assisting other employees preparing the unit for the trip northeast to Shanksville. When the vehicle was ready for departure, we were provided an escort by the Pennsylvania State Police (PSP) as a means of moving through the now snarled traffic of downtown Pittsburgh. There were vehicles traveling in every direction. The cars looked meshed like a finely woven spider web. A very intricate spider web that was tangled, yet allowed for the vehicles to pass in many directions.

As we passed along the congested roadways of Pittsburgh, I saw many a hurried pedestrian crossing the streets in between the cars and crosswalks. There were hundreds of people at the bus stops eagerly awaiting transportation that would take them home to their families and a safe place to hide. Although the traffic was jammed in every direction, the vehicle operators seemed more considerate than usual. It was as if the world had transferred all of its "rage" to a kinder and gentler personality.

The people operating their cars gave way for others in their vehicles to enter the road. The egress was slow but systematic in manner. It appeared the vibration of human nature had been changed. The routine displays of "road rage" had dissipated with the crash of the first plane as it slammed into the Tower. People now seemed to have an ability to comprehend the levels of travesty not understood before this day.

But, on this date, a time of tragedy and uncertainty, the events would linger in all of our minds forever. The balance of life once known had changed. It had transferred itself from the former level of self-preservation and moved to that of empathy for their fellow man. As we drove past so many people, their faces and clothing each different one from other, it was apparent they all shared the same look. A look of fear of the unknown and what lay ahead. It was a look I fully understood and recognized as the one which we all were wearing that day. The look resonated in the pit of my soul on 9/11 and still remains for all posterity. I stared into the crowd wishing desperately to catch a glimpse of my daughter. She was not there. I only hoped she was safely on her way home.

The trip took approximately ninety minutes to the remote landfill area of the crash site. In that time, my mind raced with questions as to what the scene would hold. Would there be any survivors? If there were, what shape would they be in? Had the scene been secured? Was there any hope for the other mothers who were waiting to find out if their child had been aboard Flight 93? Was I prepared for the momentous task ahead of me and the initial responders? Deep inside of me one of the questions was answered. I had taken an oath some seventeen years prior to protect and serve my community. This day above any in my career would determine for me if I would be capable of living up to the oath.

CHAPTER 3

A FIELD OF ANGELS: SHANKSVILLE

AS OUR TEAM NEARED THE LOCATION OF the Shanksville crash site, we observed that road blocks had been set by the Troopers from the Pennsylvania State Police (PSP). The Trooper driving our escort vehicle provided the necessary credentials for our passage. The first posted Trooper informed us that barriers had been stationed over an eight-mile radius in order to protect the scene. At this point my mind once again wondered what the crime scene would hold. If it was determined to be eight miles in diameter, there would be much to consider and plan. It became all too apparent that the primary and secondary responders to this scene truly had a very grueling task ahead. We then moved swiftly through each of the guarded barriers and continued our travel to our final destination of the crash site.

As we arrived at the crash site, the fire personnel with all of their trucks and equipment were leaving. They had just finished extinguishing the fire which had ignited as a result of the plane's jet fuel. As we drove past the vehicles with all of the personnel and apparatus hanging from the trucks, my eyes glanced at the many faces of the firefighters perched on their seats and ladders. With every new face I peered at, I thought, I saw a glimpse of despair in each set of eyes. It was in that moment I realized none of us were alone in our quest to serve. It was a comforting thought but one that chilled the very essence of my soul. If we were truly not alone, how was it possible that such a devastating incident could take place in the quiet rural area of Pennsylvania? Why couldn't so many people prevent such a travesty? It was a question which still haunts and remains with me to this day, and one in I which ponder on all too many occasion.

As we left the safety of our vehicle, we began to walk the area of the crash site. The thick smell of fuel, burning wood and smoldering pine hung low across the air and burned my nose and lungs. It was hard to breath.

In that moment, I was again reminded of my early days as a novice cop and the first time I smelled the odor of death. It is a scent which one never forgets. I was called to the home of an elderly man who hadn't been heard from for several days. His family and neighbors had made repeated attempts to contact him and were worried about his safety. As I walked onto the front porch of the home on that warm summer day with my partner, my nose caught the scent of something that I was not familiar with. It wouldn't take long to learn from the veteran officer that this was the scent of death.

When we entered the house, the smell was so intense it took everything I had not to lose my dinner. The smell of the rotted flesh raced into my nostrils and lingered there for a long time. It was an odor which never left the memory banks of my mind and will remain with me until my dying day. I recall my partner handed me a small jar of Vick's vapor rub and told me to smear a little under my nose. He explained using the rub would help eliminate the putrid odor of death. I dipped my finger into the tiny blue container and retrieved a dab of the rub. I placed the gel-like substance into the openings of my nostrils and across my upper lip area. As the eucalyptus of the Vicks permeated through my nose, my smelling sensation immediately changed. The smell of the menthol eased my fear and provided me the opportunity to focus on the task and not the foul smell.

As we began to walk the field on the warm summer day of 2001, I recall thinking that I had been to many a crime scene in my former career as a cop, but nothing had ever prepared me for this day. As I surveyed the vast scene in front of me, I felt my heart shatter and splinter into a billion pieces. The pain was so intense in the depths of my chest that I could barely catch my breath. My stomach turned at the view in front of me and I felt my soul stir in anguish. I remember being dumbfounded by the entire scene.

In my fourteen years as a police officer, I had witnessed many a malicious act, death and destructive behavior. My first big case was an armed robbery at the local State Store. This case had given me my first glimpse into the criminal mind. It had provided the beginning of my "proving ground." It would serve as my reminder of the importance of gathering the evidence. In those days of crime solving, it didn't matter what crime had been perpetrated. The crime scene had always contained a magnitude of physical evidence. There was either a weapon, some blood stains or spatters, DNA or fingerprints, a broken window, shattered glass or a severely damaged vehicle left behind. This evidence was gathered to provide the necessary information needed to solve the crime. The evidence helped to answer the many questions of who, what, when, where and why.

But, on this day, the evidence before us was not quite the same. It was not because the field was filled with carnage. It was the direct opposite. And the evidence was scattered in every direction. I was deeply disturbed by the site. Not by what was on the field, but by what was not. I was perplexed by it all. Where was the plane? Where were the bodies? Where were the remnants to remind us that these people had lived? It was as if they had been scattered to the wind.

I then felt tears well up inside me. I tried to keep the tears from falling from my eyes. I didn't want the others to see me cry. I didn't want the female in me to escape and appear weak in some way. But somehow the tears left my eyes and traveled down the pathway of my face. I tasted them and they were bitter and salty. My tears reflected the way I was feeling. I was deeply saddened over the events of the day. I was angry at this act of violence which had been perpetrated on this field. I heard my inner voice scream in agony. My first thoughts entered my mind and I heard myself whisper,

"How in the name of humanity could anyone justify killing others in God's name."

I was devastated. How had such a heinous act been perpetrated in the name of God? The God I knew would never have expected me to kill or commit an act of this nature. The God of my Bible stories had perpetuated the love of man. He had forgiven us in parable after parable. Where had the Bible indicated that this was a necessary step to gain the right to Heaven? The Bible had taught all of us to love our fellow man. There were no teachings that indicated we were to destroy each other. Whose interpretation of the Holy Word had permitted such behavior?

The God, I knew deep in the recesses of my soul, would never call for men to kill for His sake. This was not an act of honor. The God, I had read about in my youth, was one of love and kindness. After all, hadn't he given us His only Son for the betterment of all mankind? In the passages of the Holy Bible, God had told men to love and cherish others. He had told us to turn the other cheek when need be. He wanted us to live in peace and harmony with each other.

I wondered, was I the only one who felt this way or were there others who pondered the significance of these moments in time? This moment in history would be forever etched in our minds and our hearts. My heart had broken in these first minutes at the scene. My heart would remain broken for many years to come. Any innocence that had not been previously lost by earlier atrocities of life had now dissipated with my first steps onto this ground. My body heaved a great sigh and I felt the purest part of me retreat into hiding. It did not want to see all that lay before me on this field.

For as far as I could see, debris was scattered across the vast landfill. There were items not only on the ground, but also hanging in the trees. I do not know how much of what we were looking at was human remains. Or, if we'd ever be able to recover any of the poor souls who had perished on the plane. Those of us on site could see that a portion of the plane had become embedded into the ground. The soft substance of the landfill had wrapped itself around the cockpit and sucked it into its core. The ground had swallowed it up in some type of ceremonial response to the tragedy. The remnants of the plane lay on the ground in bits of cinder, reminiscent of a fragile balsa wood plane that had been laid on the ground and set fire. The forest was blackened and scarred by the events of the morning.

I peered at the scene. A whole new era of terrorism had just erupted and swept across our land. And we had just walked into a moment that would forever mark this generation and this new millennium.

I recall looking at the faces of the other FBI and the Federal Aviation Administration (FAA) personnel. I felt as if we were all moving in slow motion. Once again, I remembered my life as a police officer and all the moments spent patrolling the streets and responding to incident after incident of random violence. At times, during the heat of some scuffle, a domestic or a shots-fired call, life would begin to move in slow motion. It was as if my mind needed to slow down and remember every detail and every aspect of the others drawn into the drama. It was a means of mentally and emotionally recording the event because the need to react would take all of my energy and resources.

I felt the sun on my face. It was mid-afternoon and the sun was at its peak. But, the circle of warmth leant no comfort to the cold feeling permeating through my body. The brilliance of the sun was only an added feature of this surreal scene. We were now standing in the middle of the forest. But, there were no sounds of birds or any other animals. There was no stirring of a wind. There was only a calm silence which gave way to an eerie feeling. The feeling that I was experiencing felt similar to when I prayed. It felt as if we had stepped onto hallowed ground. A sacred place which only a privileged few would get to experience. In this moment of silence, I perceived I was experiencing one of those events in life which forever changes a human being. I sensed an epiphany. Once again, I began to pray for those lost, for their parents and families, for those of us here to assist and for those who were on their way to the scene.

We moved across the field. I was careful to respect the fact that so many lives were lost on this ground. I moved in a motion similar to a visit to the cemetery. I was very careful and deliberate in my direction as to not disturb some unseen presence. I walked over to a small rise in the ground and attempted to survey the entire scene in order to grasp, in one more fleeting moment, the magnitude of the event and our task.

As I looked across the immense space of the scene, a shimmer of light reflected off my left shoulder. The light flickered at first and played against that of the sun. I remember thinking the light reminded me of my first trip to Ireland when I saw a large school of salmon swimming very close to the water's edge. The light of their scales merged with that of the sun and sent brilliant crystal shimmers across the sky. The light was mesmerizing as I stood there in wonder. There were so many other people standing by the water watching and witnessing this natural phenomenon. It was an amazing sight and moment for me.

On this day, the shimmer of light began to grow and was almost blinding. I looked again and the light began to evolve into a foggy white mist. The white mist then began to take shape. It moved and swirled in patterns of spectacular white light. All at once, the mist took full shape and I saw what appeared to be angels. There were angels standing in the open area to the left of the crash site. There were hundreds of them standing in columns. There was a field of angels emerging from the realms of the mist. They were Archangels with their wings arched up toward the sky. Each of them appeared to be dressed in warrior garments. They were dressed like a legion of Roman Centurions from times past. The angels appeared to be ever vigilant in their gaze of the surrounding perimeter. The looks of their faces were very intense yet gentle and calming. They stood as if guarding their ground in preparation of the next battle. There were Archangels standing in the outer perimeters of the crash site surveying as if they were assessing a next move. They appeared ready for a command to march by their leader, and they clearly had a leader. He stood majestically in front of them all.

This Archangel stood with a stance of confidence and radiance. His aura portrayed that of leadership. He stood with saber in hand. The saber angled down toward the ground in a resting mode. It seemed to be an extension of his hand. I knew instantly this Archangel had to be Michael. For the Archangel Michael had always been depicted as the protector. He also was known as the guardian of law enforcement.

As I looked at these celestial beings, there appeared to be many of them. Lined up in row after row after row. They were so numerous that the images of their faces began to fade in the last of the rows. The pure beauty of the angels and the radiant light which surrounded them was overwhelming. Even though their faces and hair were different in tone and texture, each one of them was as beautiful as the other. I marveled at the image of these lovely creatures. For they were indeed an excellent depiction of the frescos which Michelangelo had painted upon his Sistine Chapel some 500 years prior.

Gazing at the angels, my mind slowed its pace and paused at each new motion made. With each movement, every detail of those first few minutes became forever etched in my memory. It seemed as if there was a sketch artist inside my mind's eye with an indelible pen weaving an artistry of design to preserve all of the minute details.

It was a remnant moment of my first big case in my earliest years of policing. My sergeant had requested I assist him with an armed robbery investigation. The actor had robbed the local liquor store and although the victims had provided a very accurate accounting of the events and had supplied an even better description of the actor there were no fingerprints or any conclusive evidence to link a known criminal as a suspect in the case. As part of the investigation, a forensic artist had sketched a likeness of the suspected perpetrator. Since there was no person identified as the actual suspect, a "John Doe" warrant was issued. A "John Doe" warrant is a document applied for and received by a judge which permits a police officer access to any known criminal or person fitting the description and/or the likeness sketched.

I was excited about the opportunity to assist in the case and grateful to the sergeant for providing me a chance to prove myself. A few months into the investigation there were still no leads to link any actors to the crime. But on one cold wintry night, we hit a "home run" and the identity of the alleged actor was resolved. It just so happened that during a routine patrol on the midnight shift I passed by a car with four males riding in it. There were two males seated in the front and two in the back of the vehicle. The car was traveling in the opposite direction from me, but my eye caught the image of the male sitting in the rear passenger seat. Within seconds, my mind clicked to the stilled image of the sketch of the suspected actor who had committed the armed robbery at the state store and it registered to the likeness of the male in the car. So I radioed for back-up and within a few minutes two other police officers were on scene. We flipped on the emergency lights and headed back in the direction of the car. We pulled it over and conducted a traffic stop. As each of the passengers was requested to identify themselves, the one male in question kept pulling his knitted ski cap further down over his face. When asked to give his name and produce some form of identification, the male became belligerent and questioned all of us about the stop. One of the officers asked him to step from the vehicle and it was then that I was sure the man standing in front of us matched the sketch and the description on the warrant. He was placed under arrest and transported to the holding cell.

To my amazement, my eye for detail had reined true and the male who we arrested bore an exact resemblance to the sketch obtained from the victimized liquor store employees. Within a short time, the male was identified, arraigned and held without bail. A few months later he was convicted on the charges and incarcerated.

I now realize that my gift for detail was indeed helpful in my chosen profession. And on 9-11, it would prove to be a gift as it was used to memorize the vision of the angels standing on the field. As my mind fell deeper into its state of oblivion over the next years, my memory sustained each and every detail of those first minutes on the field and of the angels up to and after the writing of this book.

As my mind returned back to the field, I tried to shake the vision and the image of the angels from my mind because I thought I was loosing my grasp on reality. I remember telling myself that once again my imagination had begun to play tricks on my mind. But, my trained eye stayed fixated on the image of the angelic visitors and the other faces which appeared to be a part of the entourage. I wondered, was this my mind's way of calming me as a means of preparation for the task ahead? My mind raced for answers. I had always believed in angels because my Catholicism had taught me so. My father and I had many a discussion about guardian angels and their purpose. Over the years, I believed I had seen angels. I had seen them quite often as a child and had shared this information with my father prior to his death. As an adult, especially over the last few years, I had been visited by an Archangel who always came in my time of need. He had begun to visit more often since my father's death in 1994. This Archangel was known to me as Michael. But, the celestial visitor had never appeared quite in the form which now presented itself on this field.

I began to quietly ask questions of myself. Was I really seeing angels or had my mind conjured up some symbol that would allow it to overcome the anxiety of 9-11? The voice inside of my soul which I had heard so often responded that the angels were real. The voice whispered in my ear the Archangels were there to serve and protect those souls who had sacrificed their lives for the well being of their fellow human beings. They were there to escort the heroes of Flight 93 to Heaven. Additionally, the Angels had come to protect those of us who would play a part in the investigation of this act of terror. I tried to shake the words from my mind.

At that moment, the FAA ordered all of us off the field. We were told the forest had reignited and we should also be concerned for our own health regarding the hazardous materials on the ground which we were now walking on. I began to move back toward the mobile command unit. I moved like a robot off the field, unable to respond and think about anything but the vision which I had just observed. I remember I heard what I thought was the shriek of a hawk. I turned and saw the predatory bird swooping down over the exact location where the angels had stood. I recall thinking this had been the first animal sound which I had heard since our arrival on the field. I looked again at the hawk and saw that all of the angels had now disappeared. Only the light of the brilliant sun remained. I recall praying to God to give me a sign to confirm the vision of the angels had truly happened and not just some apparition. Had he given me some marvelous gift and Blessing, or had I merely imagined it for my own comfort?

My prayer was soon answered. For on the ground, I saw a Bible lying there. It lay on the light brown sandy soil alone and away from any other remnants of the crash and the debris. It was in full view for all of us to see. One of my colleagues even commented on it. To my amazement, the Bible was completely intact. The only damage to it was that it was singed around the edges. All at once, the wind began to blow. There had been no presence of a wind prior to this time on the field. There had been no movement by anything other than those of us who stood hypnotized by the scene in front of us. As the wind whipped around us, it caused the pages of the Bible to blow open. The Bible opened to Psalm 23, "The Lord is My Shepherd." In that moment, I believed God had given me the sign I had requested of Him. It was confirmation of a miracle of a wonderful vision of His Archangels and their presence on this field of glory. God had provided me with an opportunity that few would be privileged to observe in their lifetime. Little did I know, at the time, I was ill prepared to either share the story of "amazing grace" or discuss it with others. It would take a long time before I was able to do so. But, my memory would sustain each and every detail until such time that I could reveal the story to any and all willing to listen.

CHAPTER 4

THE FIRST FEW DAYS AT THE CRASH SITE

I SPENT THE NEXT TWO DAYS CAUGHT up in a frenzy of activity, as did most others working the crash site, and felt as if I was always in an alert stage of hyper-vigilance. I helped with the coordination of the ancillary services. I drove an All Terrain Vehicle (ATV) around the landfill and delivered personnel, messages, equipment, water, food and other items needed to help prepare.

The tasks were innumerable and varied in nature. And it didn't matter at that point if it was outside the realm of an individual's usual job description because everyone working the site was willing to assist one another and help in any way possible. There was a steady stream of work being conducted on an on-going basis. And, as I stood back and watched the others at work, the flurry of activity reminded me of a busy beehive in action. Although the bees worked to achieve their individual task, they also assisted one another to meet the needs of the entire community. It was the same for all of us, as we worked in tandem to address each problem as it arose and resolve this heinous situation while recovering the remnants strewn about the dusty landfill. Each of us had our individual tasks, but was cognizant of the inter-connection of it all. We were intrinsically joined together to solve a crime and recover any traces of the victims.

Each night, I traveled back to my home, only to awaken in the morning for the journey back to the crash site. I was totally exhausted by the early morning "wake up call" of the alarm clock. The long days at the site and the return drives to my home late at night were sapping my energy and adding to the daily stress. The round trip each day was averaging about 150 miles. I would usually leave the site and arrive at home around midnight or later. With only a few hours of sleep, I would be back on the road at 6:30 AM in order to report to the site by 8:00 AM.

Those first two nights were tough on my body, mind and soul. The return home each night truly tested any ability to turn off my need to feel human. The isolation of remaining firm and in my "law enforcement zone" took every bit of extra energy that I possessed. I had to continually remind myself that "the zone" was a necessary component of my comprehension of survival. In this time of high anxiety and need for any reassurance of love, life and the return of some normalcy, it was increasingly hard to maintain control of my emotions. Especially now, that my daughter and granddaughter were currently living with me.

The two of them had been in my home for about five years. They had arrived at my home when my granddaughter was a mere nine months old. My daughter had requested to move back in with me because her relationship with the little one's father had not gone well. As she and her live-in boyfriend moved toward a parting of the ways, I was eager for the opportunity to provide her and her child a refuge. Additionally, it would give me a better chance to know my new grandchild. So, without any hesitation, I purchased a lovely red brick home just a couple of blocks away from my Mother's house and across the street from one of my brothers.

Because of my hectic schedule and traveling, I thought it would be comforting for them to have some relatives nearby. I thought the location ideal to relocate the three of us. And, if for some reason my daughter needed any help when I was not available, there were family members in close proximity to assist her and her child. But when they moved in, I was ill prepared for the emotional issues which I would have to address. After having spent so much time alone post my divorce, I hadn't realized just how lonesome I was until the first night after their arrival. As I peeked into their bedroom late on that initial night of their return, I felt my heart twist at the very sight of their sleeping faces. Once again, my maternal instincts were engaged at the thought of my girls being back at home. I welcomed the chance to become even closer in our relationship.

But now, as I walked into our home late at night, it was extremely painful to enter it while they slept in their beds. It now had a reverse reaction on my heart. And the circumstances of the current situation resulted in a stronger need for me to be with them and find a way to assure their safety and security. With our contact these last few days having been very limited to several phone calls and quick "hellos" in the morning, I longed for the touch of them and the laughter of their voices. I really needed the comfort of my family. But I knew, if I allowed myself to feel the humanity of these moments, I would have a hard time returning to my focused, trance-like state and the site. It was best that the girls were sleeping each night when I returned home. My need to analyze the vision of the angels and evaluate my thoughts would remain second to all of the other issues swirling inside my soul. My body and mind were very tired and my limited energy needed to be reserved to complete my job requirements.

In the quiet moments of those nights, I would creep inside my girls' bedroom and just watch them sleep. I enjoyed the serenity of their faces as they lay peacefully against the pillow. I relished the quiet and intimacy of this maternal world which I had been privileged to share. I would creep ever so slowly into the bedroom and immediately place my ear in close proximity to their faces to make sure they were still breathing. It was the same gesture I had completed all too many times when my daughter had been a mere babe in the crib. In the early days of her childhood, I would smooth the hair from across her forehead and place a kiss on her brow. I did this gesture in gratitude for her life and the privilege to serve as her mother.

As I watched my girls sleep, I was once again swept away to the comfort of my own childhood memories. I recalled watching my Father each night as he conducted his nightly ritual when he tucked all of his children into bed. At bedtime, he would always kiss our foreheads, brush the hair away and place a sign of the cross upon our brows. My Dad had periodically explained that he completed this ritual as a means of Blessing his children and thanking God for his parenthood. On those very precious moments of post 9-11 nights, I again felt the warmth of my Father's touch. Even though he had been dead for some seven years, I felt the gentle memories of his hand upon my brow. They tugged and whispered at the stilled remnants of him lying deep within my heart. My thoughts stirred so many memories of my Dad and how well he always protected his children. I longed for the days when I felt his touch and his comfort. I needed them so very much in these moments of turmoil. He had been my rock. He had been the anchor who had kept me fastened to the Earth. I had lost him all too soon in my life. I understood the depth of the pain to lose someone so precious. Maybe, my loss helped me to better understand the members of the victims' families whom I would soon meet.

It was amazing to me in these precious moments of our lives as parents, we see our children as the small babies who we bore and rocked in our arms. It doesn't seem to matter how old, how tall or mature that our children become. It doesn't matter that they are grown and now have children of their own. Parents regress to the simpler times when they were children. This peering and listening to the breathing of my loved ones satisfied some deep seeded maternal instinct which appeared to overwhelm me. It was a force with an unknown source that was primal and not easily explained. In this nightly ritual, the reality of the present situation of 9-11 would stir inside me. I wondered all too many times how many mothers were not going to be able to kiss their children goodnight. How many of them still did not know the whereabouts of their loved ones? How long would it take to bring some resolution to all of the mothers who had suffered? I realized how very lucky I was. I had the ability to watch my family sleep. I relished those moments and thanked God for the gift to do so.

When I would finally allow myself a few hours to relax, I found it difficult to sleep. Throughout my life, I had never been a good sleeper. Even as a child, my mind never appeared to shut down and just rest. But now, in the twilight hours of the night, I would reflect upon the vision of the angels in the field. In the safety of my home, I could ponder on the reality of what I had seen. The magnitude of each reminiscence added more detail and emotion. My mind questioned but my soul rejoiced in the possibility of what I had truly seen and in what was yet to be revealed. I had been a witness of God's benevolence. In some way and at some point in the future to come, I would be able to bear witness and give testimony of His gift to us that day.

When the mornings arrived, my mind remained in a fog. I had barely fallen asleep and it was time to awake and get moving. Despite my fatigue, I was grateful to know I would soon be back at the site, where the demands of the day would require me to once again focus on my work. My duties left little time for anything else but the tasks at hand. These tasks either great or small allowed me the chance to lose myself in a way which brought me comfort. Since my childhood, when I needed to de-stress I would clean the house and, in some obscure way, the scrubbing of the floor or the polishing of the furniture provided me with a sense of release. And in this extremely stressful time, the tasks of delivering hot coffee, meeting with the other agency reps or just talking with those most affected by the traumatic events helped relieve my tension. But each morning as I left my home and my beloved girls behind, I observed their anxiety in watching me leave and I felt it in the very pit of my soul as well.

CHAPTER 5

THE UNITED AIRLINES TEAM

ON THE THIRD DAY AT THE CRASH site, I was called to meet with a Pittsburgh Field Office Administrator who informed me that a problematic issue had arisen between the law enforcement entities and the United Airlines (UA) team. The issue was causing conflict and an immediate resolution was needed. I was advised I must immediately travel to Seven Springs Mountain Resort and attempt to mediate the matter. I was told the breach with UA appeared so urgent in nature I was to be flown by helicopter from the crash site to Seven Springs. The Seven Springs Resort was approximately 30 miles by vehicle from the crash site and had become the designated site for the coordination of all humanitarian efforts. It was where the United Airlines officials were headquartered as were all other government agency officials, medical examiners, social service providers and surviving family members of the Flight 93 passengers and crew.

A few minutes later, I arrived at the helicopter's make shift landing area. I was a little apprehensive at the aspect of flying in the helicopter. Prior to this occasion, I had experienced flying in a small craft only once before. Some twenty years prior, I had flown in a small plane with a group of friends who routinely skydived. I went to observe them jumping from the plane. It was a once in a lifetime event and I never took my friends up on the offer again. It was an experience which I did not relish ever repeating. Additionally, I was not especially fond of the idea of flying after viewing the remains of Flight 93 a few days prior. The initial memory of ill fated plane was now forever etched in my mind. I had no great urge to board the helicopter and soar into the air. As I stepped into the helicopter, I was extremely apprehensive at the prospect of the ride. The pilot greeted me and explained the flight plan and route we would take. He provided some safety tips and warned me to be very careful not to stare at the ground during the flight. He related, staring at the ground might cause me to experience vertigo. He cautioned that I should focus on looking at the horizon. The pilot also told me it would be a very short trip to Seven Springs. Before I knew it, we were hovering above the ground and heading to the Resort.

When I arrived at Seven Springs, I was led to a large room in the lower level of the main lodge. I was familiar with the room because I had routinely visited the Resort over the years to attend events such as the annual Octoberfest. Although the room was familiar to some extent, today it had drastically changed in nature. It had been transformed into a makeshift command post. Above the many tables and rows of telephones in the room, loomed signs in every direction bearing the names of various agencies. Each of the signs was hanging in particular areas of the room to indicate the space allowed for the agency representatives to be housed. In this huge room, the names of United Airlines, the National Transportation and Safety Board (NTSB), the Red Cross and other organizations hung above the floor and served as constant reminders to all about the tasks ahead. In the past, this room had been used for joyous occasions. In my experience, this room was usually filled with people, food, vendors and laughter. But, on that day, the room was quiet as people busied themselves in the manner befitting the event.

Off to the left back corner, I noticed a group of about fifteen people sitting around a large conference table. I was told this group was the UA contingency. As I approached the group, I was stopped by a tall man who presented a badge. The man identified himself as the security chief for UA. I immediately provided him with my FBI credentials. He requested to know what business I had at Seven Springs. I explained I was there to attempt to mediate the problematic issues between the UA and the law enforcement agencies. He shook his head as if he understood what I had said. He then escorted me to the group where I was introduced to a female member who was identified as the leader of those present at the table. Each of the UA group members then took turns introducing themselves and also provided me with their job titles and duties. I recall, although the group was very cordial in their demeanor I somehow felt as if I was being interrogated.

I spent about 90 minutes with the group discussing the issues. It was related to me, the primary problem which UA had with the law enforcement agencies concerned media coverage. It appeared that law enforcement was insistent about UA representatives providing information during the routine press briefings. The UA administrators believed they were not at the crash site to provide information to the media. Their primary purpose at the site was to respond and assist with the humanitarian efforts. They were there to serve in the best interest of the Flight 93 crew members, the victims and all of their surviving family members. One of the group members reminded me that UA had also suffered substantial loss of human life. The Airlines had not only lost the passengers but has also lost crew members who were their friends and colleagues aboard the fateful flight.

As we delved into our discussion about media coverage, it seemed to me there was a deeper seeded problem that no one was addressing. My intuition told me that the underlying issue was due to a breakdown in communication. Although the UA Team members and the representatives from the law enforcement agencies were focused on the same page, the two sides were missing a clear picture of each others' purpose and desired outcomes. They seemed to be confused by the meaning of the words spoken by the other. Each entity was addressing the issue in a different manner and the resulting factor had created a stalemate of sorts. The UA Team was busy addressing every detail of the humanitarian efforts and the law enforcement personnel were centering their attention on recovering evidence as a means of initiating an investigation. In the middle of all of this confusion, lay the family members of the deceased victims of Flight 93. This matter in itself was causing a great deal of grief for all of those involved at the site. The UA Team was serving on behalf of the deceased crew members, the passengers and the surviving family members. While the law enforcement professionals were focusing in on the same principle, they were going about it in a different manner thus causing a miscommunication between the two entities.

After listening intently to the concerns of the UA Team, I fully understood both sides were now divided because of a breakdown in language. This language barrier was one in which I had witnessed all too many times over my years while serving in law enforcement. There seemed to be a missing link which often set a lay person into a defensive mode. The usual response from the law enforcement officer would be an offensive stance which then caused a further riff between the two individual points of view. This language barrier was evident to me now as it had been on my very first day of policing. On that initial view into my new profession, I learned all to quickly just how little I knew about this world of my choosing. It was my first day reporting to duty and I was in the patrol car with my new partner. We were driving to the station and making small talk. As we drove down a hill, we observed a young woman jogging. She was intently focused on her motion and so was my partner. Without missing a beat in our conversation, he turned to me and said, "Nice body but no helmet."

I must have looked very perplexed at him when he uttered his words "no helmet" because he found the need to explain. He told me the woman's body was nice but her face was ugly. At that point, I was a little embarrassed over his statement and at my lack of knowledge of the lingo. I had grown up with five brothers, but it seemed I still had a great deal to learn about communicating with my fellow police officers. Over the next few years, I learned a lot about the differences in language and became better acquainted with the barriers which were created through a steady stream of misunderstood words.

As I continued to discuss the issues at hand with the UA Team, the true problem of this situation was clarified for me. Although it had a great deal to do with language, there was another equally important issue to address. The issue reflected upon the insurmountable stress levels of the UA Team who were saddened by the events of 9-11 and traumatized by their losses. To them, it appeared that their counterparts in law enforcement lacked the empathy and compassion needed to fully address the matter.

What the UA Team had initially failed to see was that the law enforcement officers were also disheartened by the events, but in order for them to handle the totality of the circumstances, most reverted back to their second persona which I have already described in a previous chapter. It is one that has been well depicted in early police shows on television. Those familiar with the original "Dragnet" series will recall Detective Joe Friday's monotone voice saying, "Just the facts Mam, just the facts." as he talked to both victims and witnesses alike. His demeanor most certainly indicated to the average person that he was indifferent to the situation and did not feel any real emotion.

In reality, he was using his defense mechanism to help him separate his emotions from the events. This mechanism is a necessary tool used to aid in sustaining the separation of heart and mind. As the left side of the brain works intensely on memorizing and analyzing all of the facts, the right side of the brain is crying out for the inhumanity of the incident or events. It is a fragile tightrope which sometimes is impossible to tread and at times, the twine leading between the two sides of the brain is frayed almost to the point of severing. This knowledge gave me the opportunity to better balance what was transpiring between the two entities. It allowed me to provide some insight to the UA Team which no one may have presented prior to this moment.

At the conclusion of our discussion, I rose from the table and extended my hand to seal the deal. As I walked toward the door, I stopped in front of an older gentlemen sitting in the corner of the room. I had noticed him upon my arrival and became aware of his presence during my discussion with the UA Team Members. On occasion, I had noticed them periodically glance in his direction. At several key moments in the conversation, the glances toward this man seemed to last for a longer period of time. At this point, I again extended my hand to the gentlemen and queried if we had a deal. The man seemed perplexed at my hand.

I then said, "It's very apparent to me that you're in charge of this group."

At my comment, he smiled and his face relaxed. He then said, "I guess you really are from the FBI. I feared that you might be a media rep trying to mislead us as a means of obtaining some information."

I too laughed and said, "If I were the media, I think I'd be much better dressed than in these dirty fatigues. I have been driving around on an ATV delivering every item imaginable and swallowing bugs at every turn. I wasn't even given any time to comb my hair or brush my teeth before I was flown here to meet with all of you."

He smiled and responded, "It was nice to see that members of the FBI had a sense of humor and hadn't forgotten how to act human."

With his last comment, I realized my hunch about the situation was right. I felt relieved to know there was indeed some hope to reduce the tension between us all. I again requested for him to confirm for me that I could report back to my supervisors the conflict between the two entities had been resolved. He indicated I could tell my supervisors that all was well, but added one stipulation. He was requesting I be assigned to serve as the primary liaison to the UA Administrative team. Additionally, he made a request for me to be housed on site at Seven Springs with the other UA personnel and the surviving family members. It was indicated this was a necessary step as a means of bettering the relationship with the UA Team who felt they were in need of constant liaisoning with the law enforcement agencies. Before I left the room, I shook hands with the gentlemen who identified himself as the Senior Vice President in charge of the humanitarian response team representing United Airlines.

In the first moments of our meeting, I instantly liked him. Despite the current situation, he displayed a warm and welcoming smile. He had a very calming demeanor. He exuded a confidence which made me feel as if everything would be okay. For a moment, the image of my deceased Dad entered my mind. I guess this man's presence had somehow reminded me of Dad, and it instantly made me feel safer and provided me with a level of comfort which I had not felt before. To this day, I am still honored to call this wonderful man my friend. Over the past years, I have been privileged to remain in contact with him and other members of the UA Team.

I left the building and was once again enroute back to the crash site via the helicopter. I returned to the crash site and updated the Field Office Administrator regarding the conversation with the UA Team. I also related the request for me to be housed at Seven Springs. Management agreed with the terms but indicated I needed to make myself available at both sites. I queried how it would be possible to travel back and forth on a constant basis. I was told to speak with the Pennsylvania State Police (PSP) Site Commander to determine if a Trooper could be assigned to assist me with the tasks ahead. Once I located the PSP Site Commander and spoke with him regarding the problem, he agreed to provide two Troopers to transport me between the two sites as well as secure any additional ancillary services needed to accommodate the UA Team.

CHAPTER 6

A MOTHER'S AGONY

ON FRIDAY, SEPTEMBER 14, THE UNITED AIRLINES Team told me about the pending arrival of a Japanese family who had lost their only son in the downed plane of Flight 93. At the time of his death, the young man was only 19 years of age. I was advised that the family was en route from Japan and was due to arrive at Pittsburgh airport sometime on the 16th. The family would then travel to the Seven Springs site via a limousine.

When the Japanese family members arrived at a private condominium in the mountains of Seven Springs, the law enforcement contingency immediately met with them. Also, in attendance were Japanese diplomats, several interpreters, and representatives from United Airlines, National Transportation Safety Board and Red Cross. Once the introductions were complete, the interpreters began to convey the family's concerns. The parents were eager to know if their son had survived and if he, or any of the passengers, had used a parachute to escape from the plane. If their son had indeed perished, the parents requested the release of their son's remains. The interpreter then indicated that the family practiced Buddhism and their religion required the immediate burial of the deceased remains.

On hearing the word "remains" uttered, the law enforcement agency representatives response to this query was quite clear. It was indicated to the interpreter there was no body to bury. The translator was advised, if there were any remains left of their son, the recovery efforts would take time. The man then passed this information onto the family. As soon as he finished with this relay, the mother's demeanor instantly changed. I watched her with great intent. Her facial features became somewhat distorted. She rose from her chair and began to scream. The tears began to pour from her eyes. It was so very apparent the extent of her agony. It was in the tone of her voice, the pitch of the scream and the emotion of her body language. She was experiencing great turmoil as indicated by the extreme emotional outburst. It was obvious that she was not only distraught about losing her son, but also about having no body to bury. There were no remains to place in the Earth and pay homage to. She would have no ability to whisper a final goodbye. She would have no opportunity to touch the face of her child one last time. Her little boy was gone and there would be no final send off. There would be no ritualistic ceremony to provide a Blessing as his soul left his Earthly domain.

In this moment of extreme emotion, I queried the interpreter. I wondered if it was an appropriate gesture in Asian culture to console the grieving mother. I did not wish to add another insult to her already damaged mind, heart and soul. The translator indicated it was permissible to show emotion and concern. I stood up from the chair and reached for her. She fell into my arms and sobbed. We walked onto the outside patio and wept. As her tears merged with mine, I realized that no common language was necessary. Even though we did not speak the same tongue, we instantly knew the others true heart. We were both aware that we shared a patois known by all mothers. It is the language of love and the dance of life between a mother and her child. Her mother's heart synchronized with mine. My mind recognized the all too familiar beating of a wounded parent who had just lost a beloved child. After all, I had witnessed this behavior in both my personal and professional lives. I had lost close family members at an early age. And, as a police officer, I had been responsible to relate to grieving family members that a child had been lost. In that instant, my mind returned to my witnessing the death of an infant. He was only nine months old and had died as a result of suffering from Sudden Infant Death Syndrome (SIDS). My partner and I received an emergency call concerning a baby who was not breathing. When we arrived at the home, the Mother met us at the door and was frantically yelling, "Save my Baby".

In the midst of her anguish, she explained that her child was not breathing. As I tried to soothe her, my partner went to look at the baby who was lying in a crib. He peered into the child and called me over. I walked over and looked inside to see a lovely little baby boy lying motionless in his bed. I could see small traces of blood coming from his nose and ears and became keenly aware of this being a sign of SIDS. I touched the child's lifeless body and it was cold. I turned to the Mother to talk and she just fell on her knees to the floor. I went to soothe her and my partner called for the coroner. I will recall to my dying day her kneeling on the floor and crying over the loss of her child. Her heart was broken and her soul cried out to God for His mercy.

Now in this time, I once again was there to help relay the devastating news of yet another of life's ironies. The law enforcement professionals were required to report the loss of this wonderful young man to his family. His life was ended along with the promise of what might have been. He was his family's hope for a prosperous future. This woman, this mother had lost her only son. The son who was her true treasure in life and the greatest of her gifts. She had once carried him in her womb and held him to her breast as he inhaled his first breaths of life. The world was now dealing her such a cruel reality. Not only had her son died, but she would not be permitted the chance to hold him once again as he took his last breaths on Earth.

To this day, my mind still travels back to a distant place and time when the rhythm of my heart was shattered in its design. It was tainted by the memory of a mother's grief, anger and a howling cry. It had been a primal scream which had rocked me to the very internal structure of my soul. This mother had been dealt the ultimate betrayal in life. She had outlived her child. She was riddled in pain and agony. A pain that was all too apparent in the irises of her eyes. She was another of the victims of Flight 93 who had penetrated the recesses of my soul. The memory of her still floods the corners of my mind. Periodically, I can still envision the look of her eyes as they pierced my own mother's heart. I wonder about her well-being and that of the rest of her family. Have they ever found any peace? My hope is this family will find some resolution in this story. Even though we do not share a common language or religion, I am hopeful we share a spiritual understanding. It is an understanding and awareness that God does exist. A God who bears a different name between us, but the same universal concept. For in the worst moment of this mother's life, God did intervene. God reached out and cared for her son when she could not. God extended His hand and brought her little boy home.

CHAPTER 7

THE DAYS AT SEVEN SPRINGS

FOR THE NEXT EIGHT DAYS, I MOVED in a mindset of oblivion. I attended meeting after meeting assisting others in arranging for the needs of the victim's families and helped ease any problems that arose. With approximately 1,200 representatives from varying agencies on site, many an hour was spent accomplishing the goals of recovering evidence, securing crime scene perimeters, interfacing with government agencies and airline administrators, arranging for additional resources and assisting in coordinating the two memorial services planned. Every one of us was engaged in a frenzy of activity and the scene looked as if it was a staged event from some cop show. It was one of those rare times when the reality of the job seemed to simulate the action of a television show, and we were all busily working the scene. We were the consummate professionals responding to our "call for service" and a myriad of personnel came from near and far to help.

At first glance, we appeared just like the archetype law enforcement professional. We assessed the situation. The site was our crime scene and it had to be secured before we could dive into our tasks. Once the perimeters were set and the Troopers were stationed to guard all of the properties from any unwanted trespassers, barriers and yellow tape were used to define the secure areas that were given limited access to only the necessary personnel. Within a short time, all on site were working in tandem and in reverence. Everyone I spoke with used the occasion to mention they too felt as if they were walking on hallowed ground and under the watchful eye of a higher power. With each comment mentioned, I stilled my consistent urge to share the vision of the angels. As the personnel began to move out across the neighborhood and community to identify any possible witnesses or additional evidence which may not have been in the immediate vicinity of the scene, we waited with baited breath for the answers to our questions. The response of the trained personnel was very precise and accurate in its design. From the outside, it may have appeared to the observer that chaos reigned. But to the trained eye, each and every person was working with a purpose to complete their tasks. The dominoes were all falling into place. It was only after the preliminary evidence was recovered that the next steps of the investigation took place to assist in painting the entire picture and drawing some preliminary conclusions to the case.

All of the personnel worked extended shifts in hopes of bringing some resolution to the unanswered questions of what happened on the plane. Were the passengers heroes and had they thwarted the hijackers attempts? Would we find any remains for each of the crew members and passengers on board? How many of the passengers and crew had left voicemail messages for their loved ones? And, if they left a message, did it contain any information that would aid in the investigation? Similar to most of the personnel on site, I barely had time to think as I moved through the motions to accomplish all of the tasks at hand. There were so many people in need of answers. All of the work requirements gave little time to sleep let alone ponder the vision of the angels.

My energy was drained. It seemed as if I had used up all of the magic of my moment which God's angels had provided. I only looked forward to my return home and the comfort of my family. Then, and only then, I might have the opportunity to sort out the mystery of that moment on the field.

On my third night of sleeping at Seven Springs, I received a call from my daughter. She sounded very distressed about some problem with my granddaughter.

My daughter told me that my granddaughter was experiencing some difficulty sleeping and had begun to regress in her daily habits. When my daughter would attempt to leave the little one at school, she would cry and panic. She was waking up in the middle of the night with nightmares and screaming out for me. When my daughter tried to talk to my granddaughter about the situation, she explained she had overheard some older children talking about the events of 9-11. The youth had spoken of Afghanistan, terrorists, bombings, fighting and thousands of dead people lying in the streets. Being only five years in age and a kindergartener, my granddaughter had become anxious about such talk. After hearing all of the chatter at school, she was now worried I was stationed in Afghanistan. She perceived me to be in the middle of some hideous battle with bodies covered in blood and scattered all around me and bombs blasting in every direction. She feared for her grandmother's safety and demanded my immediate return to her and our home.

My daughter was not sure how to explain the last few days to her child. After all, she had made a special effort to conceal all of the facts. There had been a deep seeded desire to shield her daughter from any unnecessary worry. It was her job as a mother to protect her daughter from any harm. She had kept her child from watching any network television, preferring instead to keep replaying Disney videos and other cheerful movies. She did this not only for her daughter, but also for her own benefit as well. Each day at the US Attorney's Office had become harder than the one before. The office was in chaos and the world was filled with pain and sorrow following the first few days of 9-11. She had spoken to so many people and each of them had expressed thoughts of disbelief and fear. My daughter longed for the sanity of our home. Our home was her only sanctuary. It was the last retreat. It was a place where she could hold the daughter who she loved so dearly.

I took the time to speak to my granddaughter. I reassured her that I was safe and secure. I let her know I was not in Afghanistan, nor in the middle of a battle. I explained there were no bodies lying around me and there were no bombs because I was at Seven Springs Resort. I reminded her that she had visited the Resort with her Mom and me on Mother's Day and for Octoberfest celebrations. She appeared to listen to my words and the tone of her voice seemed to calm. When I was finished speaking, she quietly asked me, "Swear to God you are okay."

I responded, "My right hand up to God."

My words seemed to relieve her worry. I assured her I would call her every night and would be home in a few more days. I requested she be kind and caring to her mother and to help take care of the family dog. I let her know of my love for her and her mother. I whispered a goodnight to her and hung up the phone. In the quiet minutes following that call, I whispered for God's help and wisdom to carry on. My heart and soul cried in silence for the warmth and comfort of my granddaughter's sweet little arms. I longed to just hold her and make her pain go away, or was I longing for my pain to dissipate with the innocent touch of a beloved child?

The first Saturday following the events of 9-11, I asked to be permitted a few hours to return to my home and was granted the leave. I had so wanted to see the girls and provide some comfort to them. I equally needed to hug and to hold them for my sake as well. Also, I had arranged to have my brother bring a friend's backhoe to dig a hole in the corner of my backyard. The purpose of the hole was to build a pond in the secluded corner of the yard and place a statue of the Blessed Mother at the top of it. I wanted to build a little grotto in which I could meditate and pray. At the time of this great need to excavate, the reason for my behavior was not yet clear. But, now I realize, I did this to help remind me of the visitation of the angels and give homage for the gifts received. In the deepest part of my soul does lie, the commitment to my religious beliefs and upbringing and it had beckoned to me to erect a symbol of my belief in the Creator. Also, to give Him thanks for the gifts bestowed. Since, I had such a meaningful relationship with the Mother Mary, I thought it befitting to have her statue near.

As I moved through the process of digging the pond's foundation and placing the stones in the form of a tiny mounted grotto, I was consumed by the need to finish it as quickly as possible. The project took a few months to complete and on the day in which Mary was placed at the top of a circular stone, I was elated to know the job was finally completed. Over the prevailing years, I have found great comfort in Her presence in my backyard. From each of the rear windows of my home, I can look out and see the lovely white cement statue with the delicate facial features which epitomize Mary's grace and elegance.

On all too many an occasion, I have walked to that corner of the yard and said a prayer on behalf of myself or for others. Each and every time, I have felt the warmth and love of the Blessed Mother's presence and comfort. When I am near the statue, I shut my eyes and I can feel her touching me, consoling my fears and anxieties. As she wraps Her white light of grace and blue robe of protection around me, I can feel my energy shift in a positive direction and my spirit come to life. To this day, my beloved Mother and friend stands in the corner of my backyard, ever watchful and ever graceful as the features of Her face are enhanced by the lovely green colorations of the plants and trees and the soft hues of the flowers. The flora and fauna of the yard are no match for the sheer beauty of Our Lady of Grace. They take form as a lovely embroidered pattern which etches the yard and only adds to the beauty of the pond. There are days when many birds gather around the statue and on occasion a brilliant red colored male cardinal perches itself on the tree above. As the red bird sings its beautiful aria into the sky, I am reminded his song reflects the thoughts of "rejoice" which I feel singing inside my heart and in my soul.

CHAPTER 8

THE MEMORIAL SERVICES

DURING THE SECOND WEEK AT THE CRASH site, two memorial services were planned and held. The first was scheduled for Tuesday and the second on Thursday. Those of us working both at the crash site and at Seven Springs were tasked to complete all of the preparations for the services. We had been advised there would be many dignitaries in attendance at the services including Mrs. Bush and Mrs. Cheney. The days prior to the memorial services were filled with innumerable meetings to discuss the event. We spent time developing an agenda and handouts for the occasion. There was a great deal of work to accomplish in very little time in order to address the needs of the family members at Seven Springs and recover the human remains at the crash site.

On Tuesday, I was requested to ride in the lead vehicle traveling in front of the buses which contained the victim's family members. The buses were enroute from Seven Springs to the crash site. As we traveled through the small town of Shanksville, the residents of the community lined the streets with American flags and waved them with such pride. There were banners which contained words of sympathy, kindness and well wishes for those seated on the buses. The residents of the community had risen to the occasion to assist their fellow Americans in their time of great need. As I peered from the marked vehicle's window, I had to swallow hard at my tears in my throat. But, this time I did not still the tears in their watery pathway down my face because I noticed I was not alone in both the tears and the heart-wrenching pain which I felt twisting in my chest. I knew this to be true, for as I looked at the face of the uniformed Trooper seated in the car with me, I observed that he too was crying. I watched as the tears streamed down from his eyes to his chin. I watched as he looked forward in an effort to avoid my eyes. He did not break his trance-like state. Even in his current state of mind of completing his duties, it was obvious that this wonderful strong man had been touched by the generosity of the residents of this small and quaint community. In this moment of solace, the Trooper confirmed for me, it was alright to cry and feel the compassion which lay heavy on my being.

On this day of all past days in my career as a law enforcement professional, I experienced my proudest moment. For as we traveled closer to the site, the Troopers representing the Pennsylvania State Police stood at full military salute in honor of the victims and their families. From the furthest security points away from the site, to the closest in proximity of the services, each Trooper stood erect and on-point. As we passed each uniformed officer, they seemed to display a paradox of emotion and demeanor. Despite their stance and current state of mind, I could see tears in their eyes. The observation of these troopers standing in a formal military ceremony honoring our fallen heros gave way to a parody of strength and compassion. Not only were the Troopers there to secure the scene and protect those around from any further danger, they were there to share their humanity with others. These wonderful men and women still remain in my mind as the epitome of self esteem and empathy. Their depiction of strength and character symbolized the American spirit and helped remind all present of the true meaning of honor.

When we arrived at the field, the Troopers in their freshly pressed uniforms lined the path leading to the crash site and paved the way for the family members to walk to the memorial service. As the family members passed by the officers, each of them proudly saluted. It was an amazing sight to see. These wonderful men and women in their pressed grey uniforms, hats and neatly shined shoes were there not only to protect, but also to provide comfort to those suffering from their immense loss and pain.

During the service, one of the deceased victim's wives had kept trying to contain her small son. It was obvious that the poor mother was very distraught with her son's behavior and her inability to control him. Just as the mother began to lose her composure and cry, a Lieutenant from the Pennsylvania State Police came to her aid. He took the small boy by the hand and led him to one of the Troopers. The Lieutenant exchanged some words with the mounted Trooper and he immediately dismounted from the horse. The Lieutenant then placed the small boy on the horse and gently guided him a short distance away from his mother and the crowd. Again, the humanity of the moment touched my heart with a wave of admiration.

These examples of kindness and compassion gave mind to the very reasons as to why most of the law enforcement professionals whom I am acquainted with answered their "call to service." And, did so with great humanity toward the victims who lost their lives and the survivors mourning their memory. They did so in the best interest of their fellow man and with such dignity.

With all of the pomp and circumstances involved with the memorial services, there were several instances which stand out in my mind. The most memorable moments were not the numerous politicians and bureaucrats delivering their speeches. They were not the diplomats who were required to be present because of the very nature of their positions. It was however the resilience of the "average citizen" who I admired most. It was the Girl Scouts who weaved red, white and blue beads onto a pin and created a symbol of the American flag. It was the school children drawing their pictures and printing their words on the colored paper to remind us of their gratitude. It was the people with their smiles, their banners and their flags which they waved with such pride. I felt such an extreme sense of patriotism as I watched the residents of Shanksville with their arms swaying back and forth with such vigor. They were there to greet and escort all of the victims' family members as they traveled toward the crash site. They were there to share their hearts and compassion with the "walking wounded" who were seated on the buses. As the people stood on the curbs and streets surrounding their homes as a tribute to the victims of Flight 93, I'm sure that the memories of their own family members stood in the forefront of their minds. Because at that moment, my thoughts turned to my own family and the longing to be near them as well.

I was also very touched by the Pennsylvania State Troopers standing tall in their uniforms as they saluted with such resolve to honor the fallen heroes. These Troopers understood all to well what it meant to pay the supreme cost to serve and protect others. By their display, it was obvious they believed each of those on board the buses deserved their tribute.

The third outstanding memory which stays contained in my mind was that of Mrs. Bush. I recall thinking upon meeting her that she was such a "First Lady." In those moments as she read her speech, it was clear she too had been deeply affected by the events of 9-11. Despite her inner turmoil, she was poised, sympathetic and sincere in the words which she shared with those in attendance. At the conclusion of the formal ceremony, Mrs. Bush lingered. She stayed for a very long while and talked with all who were present. She spent time with each of the family members who desired to speak with her. She even extended her hand to those of us working the two sites. Mrs. Bush took the time to shake our hands and thank us for all of our hard work at the crash site and in the name of the victims. By her very presence and natural ease with people, she too had served the greater good on of all who were very much in need of her comfort.

CHAPTER 9

THE RETURN HOME

I REMAINED AT THE SITE FOR TWELVE long and grueling days. Finally, on Saturday, September 23, 2001, I was going home to be with my family. I was elated at the prospect of returning. I would be able to lay my weary body on my own bed. I would be able to see my daughter and my granddaughter. I would be able to spend some quality time with them. I was hopeful that just seeing my family might help to balance my mind and soul. I wished for some control of my emotions to return.

As I opened the front door of my home, I was greeted by the smiling faces of my daughter and granddaughter and my little darling ran straight to me and laced her arms around my waist as she hugged me. We stood there for a minute and I relished the moment of my homecoming. It felt great to hold my grandchild again and to hear her express her love for me in the familiar manner we had shared. Since the time she could walk and talk, each day upon my return home, she would greet me at the door, fling her tiny arms around my legs and scream, "Situ is home."

This was our ritual and so it was on this day too. But, on this particular occasion, my eyes welled with tears at the sight of both of my girls. The touch of those small hands permeated through my skin and traveled to the very core of my heart and soul. I was elated to be home and grateful to have the fortune of reuniting with my family who had been safely nestled here amidst so much tragedy.

As I knelt down and hugged my lovely little creature, my mind returned to the vision of the many grieving family members whom I had met at Seven Springs. Each of their faces was scanned in the memory card of my mind. Each of their stories was forever etched in the tunnels of my ears. Each of their deceased family members walked along the trenches which led to my tattered soul.

The memory of all of this has been forever drawn inside me like a finely detailed sketch. I can still recall my first glance of the field at Shanksville and wonder how long it will take for that memory to go away. Little did I know the image would never leave me and only grow more vivid with each passing year. In the aftermath of the horrific events of 9-11, the crash site, the victims' family members with their individual stories of loss, the memorial services and all of the stress, it was astounding to me that the robotic trance which had taken hold some two weeks prior had been stilled by the very touch of my granddaughter's tiny hands. It felt symbolic in its approach, for as her hands wrapped around my body, I felt my heart melt at the sensation of her fingers pressing against my legs. In all of the years of law enforcement, I had wrestled with the transition of the two personalities contained inside of me. But now, on this day, I became aware of all it would take to change me from my superwoman persona was the simple touch of a loved one. It was then I truly understood the meaning of the power of love.

Later, that evening, as I sat down on the couch in the seat which my family had designated as mine and cherished the moment of us all being together. It had felt like a lifetime since we got to interact as a family. How wonderful it was to be with them again. I relished their presence and enjoyed the warmth of our home. I smelled the familiar fragrances of the room. I saw the family photographs lined so neatly on the wall of the stairwell. I smiled at the familiar faces and poses of my family which lit the recesses of my mind. I touched a photo of my Dad and said a silent prayer. The glass and the gold frames gleamed against the mirrored light of the sun. How simple it all seemed. These were the thoughts that had sustained me through the last few weeks. I had all of the important pleasures in my life. I had the love of my family and the Blessings of my home. How many of us had taken all of these things for granted prior to 9-11. My Father had always called me a simpleton. It was a term which I had not quite appreciated being called in my youth. Dad had always indicated I took delight in the smallest of things. Now, in these initial days of post 9-11, I took great pleasure in the return to my girls and this tiny home set on the hill above the Allegheny River.

I was only home for a few hours when my granddaughter demanded to know more about the Seven Springs Resort. I tried to explain to her once again that she had visited the Resort with me on several occasions. However, try as I may to convince her the spot had been a safe haven, she refused to believe me. She insisted I was not being truthful with her. As I watched her debate the issue with me, I realized she too had been traumatized by the events of the past few weeks. Even though she had been sheltered from all of the daily news releases, she had still been touched by what had transpired and what she had heard. She had listened to the whispers of other children recounting stories from countless newspaper articles. All of the adults around her had been incapable of shielding her from the hardships of 9-11.

I decided there was only one way to resolve my "standoff" with the youngster. I told my daughter to pack a bag for my granddaughter because we would be traveling back to Seven Springs, together. I explained it was the one true way for the little one to understand. She needed to see the Resort for herself and walk the surrounding properties to be assured I had been safe. It would be the only way for her to fully comprehend that the nightmares she was experiencing were images she had created based on limited information she had received from the older children. I made a quick call to the front desk of the Resort to arrange for a room. We got into my car and traveled to Seven Springs.

On the drive up, I had to continually reassure my granddaughter we would be safe and no harm would come to either of us. The ride seemed to take longer than it had over the past two weeks. I realized I was driving at a much slower pace than normal. I took note I always seemed to slow down when the little one was in my car. Before too long, we arrived on the Seven Spring's properties. Although it was night, the lights in the parking lot illuminated the areas around the Resort and provided an opportunity for us to see the many buildings and grounds. As we looked across the vast areas, my granddaughter appeared to become more peaceful. The once taunt muscles of her mouth and forehead relaxed and eased away the frown. She turned to me and smiled. She then said, "So, this is where you stayed."

I responded, "Yeah, so this is where I stayed."

We entered the building and walked around without saying another word. Before too long, we met up with some of the remaining United Airlines personnel who had not yet left the site. We sat for a while and talked with the others. It wasn't too long afterwards, my granddaughter laid her head on my lap and feel asleep. My heavy heart filled with such warmth and emotion. I captured the moment in my mind's eye and whispered my thanks to God. I was grateful for this return to my life. It was a reminder that I had a wonderful life. It was full of significance and family to love. It had a purpose and I was truly blessed. I then lifted my granddaughter from my lap and carried her to our room. We spent a quiet and uneventful night at the Resort sleeping. As the memories of 9-11 swept through my mind, I found some peace lying next to this child. She was my life and my future legacy. As I listened to the quiet snoring of her breathing, I feel asleep as well. It was the first real rest I had since that fateful morning of September 11.

CHAPTER 10

THE RECKONING BETWEEN MIND AND SPIRIT

IT WOULD TAKE A FULL YEAR UNTIL the time of the first anniversary of 9-11 for me to come to grips with the vision of the angels on the field. As a means of remembering those who perished during the traumatic events of September 11, a memorial service had been planned at the crash site in Shanksville. It was my intention to attend the memorial service and visit with those whom I had spent so much time with during the initial days of post 9-11. I also intended on revisiting the site where I first saw the angelic vision.

I arrived at the site with great apprehension and anxiety. I had not slept the night before and my exhaustion was not helping my mood. As I walked through the crowd, I saw so many familiar faces. Some of those in attendance were victims' family members and some were the representatives from United Airlines and the government entities I had worked with some twelve months prior. It was good to see all of those persons whose faces pierced the memories of my mind when I would dream at night. I spent a few moments conversing with many of them, anxious to hear their updated news. I then took a brief stroll to look at the site and I attempted to retrace my steps from the year past. But the ground did not look the same. With all the throngs of people, spectators and the media walking the grounds, I became disoriented in my direction.

My attention was then drawn to the memorial service which had just begun. Despite the fact the day was a somber event and the weather was somewhat overcast, the pomp and circumstance of the moment was elegant and the service was beautifully staged. I listened to the service ever cognizant of the vibrations around me. I kept looking and hoping for a second opportunity to see the angels again, and I made a silent prayer for God to give me a sign to validate what I had seen on my first visit to this site. It wasn't too long before my prayers were answered, and I received my sign. During the ceremony, as the voices lifted in a solemn song, a wind ripped through the field and it reverberated off of the make-shift theatre's metal roof. It echoed loud and hard. For a brief moment, all were silenced as the mighty wind echoed through the amphitheatre. All at once, the music sounded and eased my mind of the memories of a burning plane. The wind blew and cleared the pain. The voices of the family members who were present reminded me I was not alone. In that precise moment in time, I remembered we are never truly alone. As fast as the wind came in and blew across the crowd, it was gone. Once again, I believed my answer was clear. It was true. I really had been given a Blessing. I had seen God's Angels walking the Earth on one of the worst days in American History. I had been honored and privileged to witness them. I now wondered "why me".

Later that evening, in the still of the night and in the quiet of my home, I reflected on the events of the past year. Over the year, I had wondered all too often if I had indeed lost my mind on 9-11. I felt so isolated and alone. I knew I had to talk to someone and very soon. As I pondered the dilemma of who to confess to, my mind began to hear the words of a poem. Through the years, I had often written poetry in troubled times of my life.

I wrote down the words of this poem and put them away for safe-keeping. I placed them in a book. A book I did not return to until August of 2008. I came upon the poem when I was sorting out my book collection in an attempt to better organize them onto shelves in the upstairs bedroom of my home. The poem was kept alongside some notes which read, "my life's plan."

The poem read as follows:

I said goodbye today
It didn't remove the pain
It didn't remove the memories
Not the good not the bad
The goodbye brought me no closure

I said goodbye today
To my past, to my present and to my future
I let go of all my dreams
I let go of all of my wonder
I said goodbye today
While a distant trumpet played
While the sighs, the tears and the words
echoed across the sky
As I stood in silence searching for one face
for one spirit to rise from the plain

I said goodbye today
In an open space of time
In a field sometimes forgotten and filled
with unknown names

Not kindred to warmth
Not kindred to the rhythm of my soul

I said goodbye today…

In retrospect, I realize the poem had some truth to it. I may have said goodbye, but I had not eradicated the pain from my thoughts, feelings or emotions. I merely allowed it to become buried deep inside my heart, my mind and my soul.

CHAPTER 11

FIRST CONFESSION

A FEW DAYS PASSED AFTER THE FIRST anniversary event and I finally made the decision with whom I should speak. Because of my Catholic upbringing, I needed to seek the counsel of a priest. I felt the desire to reach out and confess. I was in so much turmoil about the situation. And all of the mistakes I had made throughout my life had somehow made me feel less than worthy. It seemed I had dwelled on the negative aspects for so long, I had no real ability to see the positive and my path back to my inner beauty. I could not see myself for the kind and caring person I was. I wondered why I couldn't extend the same courtesy and compassion for myself that I had for others in my life. It seemed my strict Catholic upbringing gave me little ability to forgive myself for any of my past trespasses. These feelings of unworthiness only compounded my anxiety and caused me to feel less than the appropriate recipient of God's amazing gift. In addition to these feelings, I wanted so much to share another secret with the priest which lay hidden in my mind and soul.

Since childhood, I had seen the vision of St. Michael the Archangel. On occasion, Michael would appear and whisper in my ear some words of wisdom or of a cautionary warning.

Although I had firmly believed the Archangel was present in my life, I had rarely spoken of his existence. As a small child, when I would mention the angelic viewing to a family member, I was reprimanded and the vision was pushed away as some imaginary childhood manifestation. So, my hesitation in revealing this story of a field of angels was even more justified in my mind and validated in my heart.

As I grew into adulthood, the visions of Michael and his whispers in my ear continued. But what had transpired in my mind as I advanced in age was the assumption the visitations by angels were only granted to the privileged few on Earth who had lived some devout and chaste life. In my mind, I had learned about life through a series of hard lessons only after living and breathing too many mistakes. I kept pondering all the people whom I believed would be more worthy than the likes of me. I did not feel I had earned such a Blessed gift. Because of these feelings and a need to understand the purpose of the event, I decided it was now time to share with another person my amazing story of grace. Of course, I hesitated not knowing if it was a prudent decision to discuss my vision with anyone else. I questioned who it should be. If I told someone at work, I was sure they would think I had suffered some trauma to my mind. If I told my family, they too may feel my mind had succumbed to some emotional stress post 9-11. I decided to talk to a priest, a man who had become a friend and my spiritual counsel and one of the few people who would be sworn to secrecy by his very vows of silence.

A day later, I called my friend, the priest. I knew him to be the right choice for me because I had trusted him before when I was in need of spiritual counseling. When I heard his voice, I became very emotional and almost found it impossible to speak. As I regained some composure, I requested a meeting to discuss a problem and he was willing to talk and try to help me. When we met a few days later, I revealed to him my story of the angels. He listened very intently and thanked me for the privilege of sharing the ominous event with him. I related to him I was deeply troubled by two issues. Had my mind played tricks with me or had I really seen a vision? And if so, why me? I had not lived the life one would perceive as a person which such a Blessing would be bestowed. I was not devout like others I knew. I had made so many mistakes in my life and did not feel I had made atonement for them. This priest explained God had provided me this Blessing because he did not look at me as a sinner. God looked at me as one of His children. He had forgiven my trespasses and now he was telling me it was time for me to forgive my sins. He was giving me the grace to move forward and share this miraculous story. God wanted others to know He was there on that fateful day. He sent His angels to recover His children who had lost their lives in His name. At that moment, I knew the priest was right because I was filled with such hope for a new beginning. It was time to move on with a life which would now be filled with "light".

At the conclusion of our discussion, I realized the magnitude of his words. It matters not of my stature in this life. I am not queen, king, aristocrat or even a president. I am clearly not perfect in my humanity or personality. I am like many others who were alive on 9-11. I am an imperfect child of God who has made many errors with my choices and, on occasion, my lifestyle. However, the only mistakes which matter are if I have not learned. Oh, and I have learned. As a small child, from time to time, my Father would read to his ten children from the Bible. I recall once at the age of about seven or eight Dad read the Ten Commandments out loud. At that tender age, it seemed like a lot of information to digest.

When my Dad was finished reading, I said to him, "Daddy, I'll never remember all of those rules".

My father responded, "Lillie Marie there are many rules to remember. But, if you live your life with one basic rule of trying never to intentionally hurt another person, then you are following God's commandments."

At that time in my life, I had little comprehension of my Dad's words. But after listening to my priest's comments, I had some clarity and knowledge of their meaning and as to why God had chosen me to deliver this story of His angels. It did not matter about my mistakes. In some profound way, by serving as a law enforcement officer, I had made my atonement to God. It was obvious that God had forgiven me. Now, it was time for me to forgive my own trespasses. But, how could I achieve forgiveness for a lifetime filled with mistakes.

I then realized that forgiveness is the true essence of life. It is a passage which is necessary to attain. It quakes the very core of our being. It is a sustaining package of time, mood and reason. Forgiveness of self for wrongs committed against others is essential to move forward on the path of reckoning. I had been held hostage in the gathering of life's atrocities as they merged into an organism of one. All of the memories and pain lit my mind with this cataclysmic event and festered deep inside. It was not possible to move forward with my life if I could not first let go of the past. To achieve a state of forgiveness, I had to transfer my thoughts from the negative manner I had become accustomed to. I had to achieve a higher level of thought.

In those moments of remembering the words of my beloved Dad, I had been able to recapture my heart's content. Forgiveness had provided a spiritual renewal. It had allowed my soul to soar to new heights. It had expanded my mind in ways I would never have imagined. The forgiveness attained for myself and for others had helped the malady to heal. The malignancy which had weighed me down for so many years had drifted into the oblivion. Oh yes, the forgiveness came in the recall of not just the past deeds, but for time served in the protection of others and that of my country.

CHAPTER 12

A REFLECTION OF MARY MAGDALEN

IN THE DAYS THAT FOLLOWED MY CONVERSATION with the priest, the impact of the discussion took a few days to truly sink in. On one particular evening, I was attempting to collect all of my thoughts and finally analyze them. As I worked through some facts, my thought patterns began to reflect the recollection of a book. My mind recalled a book which my Dad had given to me. It was a book entitled: "Jesus the Son of Man" and it had been written by Kahlil Gibran, the Lebanese Prophet. The book provided Gibran's interpretations of Jesus's first meetings with some of the most significant persons in His life. One of the passages in particular had caught my eye so many years prior. It was the story of Mary Magdalen and her first encounters with Jesus. Now, in these moments of reflection, I understood the relevance of self forgiveness and change. After all, Mary Magdalen had changed her life upon her first encounter with Jesus. Because Jesus had seen her true essence and the beauty that dwelled in her soul, He forgave her. His love for Mary Magdalen gave her permission to love herself. In that instant of recognition by Jesus, her heart opened and she changed. She changed her image to reflect Jesus's light.

All my life I had a special relationship with the two Marys of the Bible. I adored both Mary the Mother of God and Mary Magdalen. I had prayed to Mary Our Mother of Perpetual Help since the birth of my daughter. On the morning following her birth, my Mom gave me my first prayer book which honored the Mother. From that moment on, I dedicated my heart to Mary and prayed to our Lady on a daily basis. In the months following 9-11, I built a shrine to pay homage to Mary in my back yard. I did so as a means of comfort and to remind me I had been delivered. On every single morning since Mary's statue was mounted atop a small pond that I called "the grotto", I have knelt to pray to her. Each day that has since passed, I have bent down and bade her a good morning and a good night. I have repeatedly uttered the same words as I open and close the blinds. I say to Her statue, "Good morning my beloved Mother and friend."

These two women with uniquely different lifestyles shared the love of a man. One shared Jesus's life as His Mother and the other shared it as his devoted colleague and friend. One of them was pure and chaste and the other was free spirited in nature and worldly. As a woman, I reflect the traits of both. My inner soul reflects the purity of Mary for her son. I understand her acceptance of a child into her life at an early age. I too share the knowledge of Motherhood and its bond to the universal energy.

My humanity also reflects the imperfection of a woman. I was and still am a woman who has made mistakes in her life. Like Mary Magdalen, I too have lived a lifestyle of pain. I have reveled in the shadow of the admiration of men. I have made choices I am ashamed of. These choices did not help or inspire me to become a better person. On the contrary, some of my choices almost bound me to a negative path and behaviors.

I found little comfort in forgiveness of myself or others. Yet, despite those mistakes, post 9-11, I have clearly chosen a new path of genuine enlightenment.

In this newly found knowledge, I realized God had provided me with a gift. He had given me His Divine Grace. He had peered inside my being into the recesses of my heart and soul. Inside my heart, God had found its sheer purity. He had located my inner perpetual light just as He did with Mary Magdalen. It was a lovely pure light which sustained itself despite the harsh realities of life with all its difficulties and temptations. It was this purity of heart and the strength of my beliefs that allowed me to finally accept His gift.

Our beliefs matter the most. Our beliefs move us to accept our inner being and strength. Our beliefs whisper the words which allow us to take the right action on behalf of ourselves and others. Our beliefs allow us to trust. This trust guides our path. My path has been a long and arduous journey. It is a personal pilgrimage which I would gladly embrace again. For in this odyssey of discovery and retribution, I have been able to achieve a positive outcome. It is an outcome of knowledge that God is here. He is in the essence of the warm morning sun as it gazes down upon His Earth. He is here in the faces of His people as they turn to look toward Heaven. It is here in the laughter of His children as they dance and sing His praises. It is here in His kindness and grace. His grace was here on that fateful day of 9-11. God extended His hand to His children and I was privileged to witness His "field of angels." I was there as a witness and to bear testimony of His benevolence.

CHAPTER 13

A TRAUMATIC INJURY

IN JUNE OF 2005, I BEGAN TO experience some severe health issues which resulted in additional stress for me. I spent months visiting doctors trying to determine the cause of my illness. My primary care physician had indicated she observed a decline in my health since my involvement at the Flight 93 crash site. She advised me that she believed I had been traumatized in some way and my autoimmune system had been directly affected by the additional stress of the event. The doctor recommended I see several specialists in order to determine my present condition.

Although, the symptoms I was experiencing were wide spread throughout my body, I was beginning to see a clear pattern. It seemed any stress would cause the onset of high anxiety. Then, a painful migraine would begin in the mid-point area of the back of my head and my entire body would begin to stiffen from the effects of the pain. Sometimes, I felt like someone had placed a steel girdle to the interior of my body and kept pulling it tighter and tighter until I was unable to breath. The whole time I could feel the rapid firing of my adrenalin repeatedly sending those signals of "fight or flight" to my brain. When the chest pains started, I felt my first glimpses of a fear of dying.

But, it was the anxiety attacks that worried me the most. I couldn't stop the profuse sweating, the hyper-breathing or the adrenalin rushes that surged and cycled through my body. It was in these times I felt the most vulnerable and had no real ability to reason or contend with any situation that arose. When I look back at what drove me to see the doctors, it was because my daughter kept pointing out the change in my behavior and emotional responses. She had repeatedly told me I was over anxious about the simplest of situations. She felt I continually overreacted to the most minor events in our lives. As a result of my daughter's continued concern, I sought out the advice of medical professionals and scheduled appointments with the recommended specialists. When I look back on this period in my life, I am grateful for the grace which was bestowed upon me because without it I'm not sure I would have survived to share this story of God's love.

After a few months and all too many doctors' visits and a series of diagnostic testing, I was told I was suffering from Post Traumatic Stress Disorder (PTSD). Each of the doctor's had indicated that stress was the only clear reason for my experiencing my present health difficulties. The testing had ruled out any other major contributing factors. Each of the physicians believed the diagnosis to be PTSD. At that particular time in my life, I had an extremely hard time accepting their diagnosis. After all, I had always been a Superwoman. I was strong and invincible and capable of handling any problem. I had accomplished a great deal in my life and weathered many a storm. I didn't have the time to address such matters. I hadn't allowed myself to feel as most women did. I had hidden my feminine essence as a means of self protection. My job had not permitted me any close involvement to those victimized or in need. Nor, was I permitted any emotional displays which would indicate my gender. I was trained to "tap down" all of my thoughts and feelings. I was there merely to serve and protect the greater good of my fellow man.

This need to suppress my true feelings came as a result of my role as a "spectator" in my new world of the "testosterone jungle." I had placed the special part of my femininity in a secret hiding place. The deeper I secured the female in me the more I forgot who I was. I became immersed in this new identity and firmly believed this change in me was precipitated by an incident which took place in the early stages of my career.

On a quiet Sunday evening, in the first months on the job, I was dispatched to assist with an emergency call received regarding a vehicle accident with injuries. The dispatcher indicated the accident had taken place outside of a local church located in the neighboring community. The church in question just so happened to be the one my family had attended for several generations. When I heard the call, I immediately responded. As I arrived at the accident scene, I observed a vehicle had struck a very large tree which was located in an adjacent parking lot to the church. The vehicle was badly damaged and as I approached the car, I saw there was an elderly female lying on the street. She was barely moving and it was obvious she was gravely injured. I rushed to her and it was apparent she had multiple injuries to her body and her breathing was very labored and raspy.

As I lifted her into my arms, I noticed there was another woman still seated inside of the car. I could only see the top of the woman's torso for the rest of it was hidden under the vehicle's dashboard. It appeared the impact was so great that the front end of the car had collapsed around the poor woman. As I looked even closer at the two injured females, it was then I recognized them. They were the two elderly sisters who had been consistent parishioners of the church and had usually sat in the front pews on any given Sunday Mass. I remembered noticing them on many an occasion when I had attended a service. Week after week, they were seated in the same pew and dressed in a lovely fashion. Throughout my years as a child, I could recall their "ladylike" attire quite well. Each of them usually wore a pair of gloves on their hands and a hat on their heads and were always well-mannered.

As my mind returned back to the scene, all of the emergency personnel were now responding. Several police officers had arrived as did the firefighters and the emergency medical personnel. As I watched the firemen begin to extricate the woman from the car, I could hear the other woman's breathing becoming more labored. She was bleeding from several locations and had bones protruding from parts of her arms and legs. And, as I held her in my arms, I prayed for her well-being. I tried to speak to her and attempted to soothe her as well. But, I noticed that she was now unconscious and I was grateful for her reprieve from the pain. In a few minutes, the parish priest arrived and began to administer "last rights" to her. As the priest anointed her with oil, my heart was moved by the very essence of the ritual and I found it hard to stay detached from all that was taking place. I had never before observed such an anointing and I was overcome by the thoughts of another human being dying in my arms.

It was then I noticed the many spectators watching the events taking place and my heart cried out for the poor woman to be given some privacy. My mind could not fathom why any one would desire to stand and watch another person suffering in such a manner. As my mind tried to keep control of my emotions, I felt my eyes fill with tears. In that moment, the grief I felt became too much and I began to cry. As the tears streamed down my face, I heard one of the firemen say to me, "You see this is why we don't want any women working as a police officer. A woman can't do the job. Men don't cry while they are working and women do."

When the fireman finished making his comments, I heard one of my fellow police officers respond to him, "She is doing her job and at the same time showing compassion for someone who is obviously dying. Be quiet and let her alone. She is a good officer and I'm proud to work with her."

Without another word being said, all of the responders continued in their efforts to sustain the lives of the two women. However, within a brief moment's time, the woman lying in my arms succumbed to her injuries and strained to give one last breath. As she stopped breathing, I realized that someone had died as I held them in my arms. The tears for the loss of her flowed in a steady stream and my heart ached for the life which had now ended. The medical personnel took her from my arms and placed her on a gurney and within a few minutes she was covered with a white blanket and placed inside the ambulance.

At that moment, I realized the gravity of the work I was now involved in. It was going to be more then just responding to some routine call for service. There would be times when someone's life lay precariously in my hands. I wondered was the male firefighter right? Was my gender a hindrance on the job? Before I could further question my capabilities, the second woman was being extricated from the car. As the fire personnel lifted the dashboard from the woman's body, she screamed in pain and all present turned to look in her direction. It was then I noticed her leg had been severed at the thigh and she was profusely bleeding from the injury. As the emergency responders worked to aid her, she fell unconscious and I was grateful for the fact that she could no longer feel her pain. I can still vividly recall the sight of her injured limb. It was the first time I had ever seen such a wound. The memory of her still lies in the chapters of my mind.

This accident was one of the first tragedies I ever witnessed up close and personal. It was also one of the initial exposures to men who questioned my ability to work as a police officer while responding to a call for service. In retrospect, I occasionally think of the male officer who rushed to aid me. He provided some strong words of wisdom to not only the firefighter, but to me as well. He gave me the approval I needed not only as a woman but as a rookie cop. Although he had reassured me it was alright to feel human as I conducted the required duties of a police officer, inside my mind I knew it would be the last time I would cry at the scene. My ego would not permit it to happen again especially not in front of the men. And, over time, my ego would not disappear or budge on its unemotional stance. To the contrary, with each passing year in the law enforcement profession, it grew stronger in its identity and became more of an ingrained part of my anatomy. It had a life force of its own and one which deeply affected my ability to reason with myself as it related to my health issues in the present time.

For over two years, I ignored the PTSD diagnosis. Then, in the Fall of 2007, I found my original notes from Flight 93 and my world as I knew it came crashing down around me. I happened to come across the notebook while cleaning my office inside the FBI complex. I was cleaning out my space with the intention to resigning my position and leaving the FBI. I was in so much turmoil and was having a tough time making decisions about my life on a daily basis. It was becoming increasingly difficult to hide my physical symptoms and ease my anxiety.

It was a Friday afternoon and I remember telling myself I would pack the notebook in my case and take it home. I had every intention of reading it that evening. At the conclusion of my workday, I traveled home and anxiously awaited the opportunity to look at my notes. Once at home, I eagerly opened the notebook and began to read through it. To my surprise, I was immediately transferred to the crash site. It was as if no amount of time had transpired. I was surrounded by the trees and the other settings of the field. I saw the image of the hole where the plane had sunk into. I saw the ponds filled with the water and debris. I remembered the many faces of the firefighters with their tarnished faces looking at me with no emotion. I began to feel highly agitated and claustrophobic. I then experienced a kaleidoscope of emotions that ended with my sobbing. I heard myself wail and yell with anger. It took me a few minutes to realize I wasn't at the crash site, but sitting in my bed. I then became so ill I had to remain in bed for two days.

A few days following this episode with the notes, I had a scheduled appointment with my primary care physician. As she sat next to me and queried the state of my health, I apologized to her for my inability to accept her diagnosis. She inquired what had brought this epiphany to me. I explained about reading the notes and the resulting health issues. I told her I realized that my resistance to her diagnosis of Post Traumatic Stress Disorder (PTSD) was the result of my ego. Until that time in my life, I hadn't quite understood just how huge my ego was. It ruled me in some ways. It had found a home in my stubbornness and strength. It had dug its roots deeply into the trenches of my mind and would not give any ground. She laughed at me and then her eyes welled up with tears. The Doctor then said to me, "Your best personality traits are also your worst."

I laughed at her and replied, "Since I was a child, I have always been told that I'm my own worst enemy."

How true I now understood these words to mean. I had a tough time trusting myself and others too. Trust is a multi-faceted word which bears true meaning in hidden ways and dimensions. As a child, so many years prior, my trust had been annihilated. I had been sexually abused by a trusted adult. He had not only robbed me of my innocence. But, he had tortured my heart, my mind and my soul. What he had robbed from me all of those years ago, had taken great effort to regain. The many years of life that followed the abuse only added to my pain and sorrow. The abusive incidents had left me with such self doubt about my ability to allow myself to fully trust another human being. Each time I had attempted to reach out to another, I would retreat to a safe haven. There in my domain, I would remain and not allow any one a pathway into the internal structure of my heart. I would only permit some momentary glimpse at life's promise. After all wasn't that why I had become "Superwoman." As Superwoman, I wouldn't need to rely on anyone else's help. I would be invincible and self sustaining. I would be able to defeat any foe or rid myself of any problem. Boy, did I need a reality check and it had arrived. It had announced itself in the form of illness. I had brutalized my mind so much that my body now reflected the ravaging of my soul.

CHAPTER 14

THE FLASHBACKS: A RETURN TO THE SCENE

A FEW DAYS FOLLOWING THE INCIDENT WITH the notebook I experienced another flashback. I was at the gas station and was standing in close proximity to a man putting diesel gas into his pickup truck. I inhaled some of the fumes of the gas and was again transferred to the crash site. I was in the mobile command unit and arriving at the scene. The firemen with their equipment were just leaving the site. The burning smells of fuel and pine entered my nose. The world stood still for a few moments and I remembered the field. It was as if the universe had elapsed time and I had been once again placed on that field. I was destined to relive the surreal scene again and again and again. It took a few moments to regain my composure.

It was only after these two experiences in reading the notebook and the flashback that I accepted the diagnosis of PTSD. A few weeks later I had another visit with my primary care physician, at which time I once again apologized to her for not accepting her original diagnosis of PTSD. I related to her the events of the past few weeks. My doctor was elated at my final acceptance of the diagnosis. She felt that it may be a turning point in my healing process. She explained my inability to accept the diagnosis was similar to those suffering from alcoholism. She related that as long as I denied my condition there would be no ability to treat it appropriately. Now, that I had stopped denying the diagnosis and my worsening condition, I would be better able to respond to treatment.

On the day of my third granddaughter's baptism, I experienced another flashback. This one was even more worrisome than the last two. It resulted as the priest was giving his sermon regarding the significance of baptism. The cleric related his interpretation of the crucifixion of Jesus. He indicated according to the Bible the Earth quaked and the ground opened up as Jesus died on the cross. When the Earth opened, all of the Saints arose from the ground. He explained the Saints had arisen in reverence to the Son of God's death and His extreme sacrifice to mankind.

As the priest uttered these words, my mind again traveled to the crash site and the field of angels standing and waiting. I viewed them in all of their revelry and splendor. They stood tall, strong and ever vigilant. It was as if I was there at the crash site again. I felt all of the emotional sensations of that day of 9-11. I became extremely disoriented and did not fully comprehend where I was. I felt all of the others around me in the pews. But, at the same time the surroundings of the crash site were there too. I panicked at my recollection of those first moments on the field. It took me about three to four minutes to come back to reality. I was standing in the church and my family members were all around me. How real the flashback had indeed felt. I had relived it in my mind's eye. I once again saw all of the same sights, smells, the confusion, but not the other people. In this flashback, I was at the scene all alone. I stood in the middle of the field and felt myself swirling. I looked across the pond and saw my angels standing there. They were there just as they had been on 9-11. I began to cry and the tears started running down my face. It was in that moment my eldest granddaughter took notice of the tears and placed her hand on my arm as a means of her endearment. At that point, I was brought back to the present time. And, just as her touch had brought me back to reality post 9-11, it appeared it had allowed me to return to the church and my family. I had traveled back to the sights and sounds of the present day. I had returned to those I loved. It was so extremely difficult to focus. But, I smiled at her and I attempted to regain my composure. When she asked, "Are you alright?"

I answered her by saying, "My tears were those of joy and not of pain."

Upon my explanation, my dearly loved granddaughter just smiled and moved toward me to snuggle.

The rest of that Sunday moved in oblivion. This of all days should have been one of complete joy. The family had been once again blessed by the newest granddaughter. It was supposed to be a day of celebration. I tried to compose myself and appear as if all was well. But, as the day passed, I could feel the tremors inside my body. I knew it was going to be a rough day and even a tougher night ahead. I knew there would be no rest.

I spent the night lying in bed and trying to sleep. My body was so restless and my mind was given no reprieve from its constant thoughts. The tremors inside my body gave no way to allow for a peaceful refrain from its present state. The tremors always scared me. They were so unsettling. During those moments, my fear always heightened. I had no control of my body nor would it respond to my will. I hated the night. I longed for the soft-spoken words of comfort from my Father. I needed him so desperately. I needed him to tell me that all would be well soon. My pain was unseen but, yet so deeply seeded inside of my being. I longed to scream aloud and tell everyone of my hurt. If only pain was apparent, the outside world could view for themselves the magnitude of my wounds. It would be so very obvious to all that I was deeply injured by my experience at Flight 93. I had been rendered silent by the enormity of the scene and by my inability to tell the world of the angels in the field.

CHAPTER 15

A SPIRITUAL SURRENDER

THE DAY FOLLOWING THE FLASHBACK IN CHURCH I again became very ill. I experienced high anxiety and hyper-vigilance. I lost focus of my day-to-day tasks. I was so upset at the occurrence of the flashback that I contacted my physician to seek counsel. I also spoke to my priest and told him about the flashback incident. I spent the next five days trying to revive my body and my mind.

It was one week later after experiencing the flashback that I finally comprehended the message I was meant to understand. The message was symbolic in nature. I believed that the passengers and crew members of Flight 93 had sacrificed their lives just as Jesus had sacrificed himself for the benefit of mankind. In those first moments on the plane, the passengers and crew were not aware of the hi-jackers plans of destruction or their final destination. However, they were knowledgeable of the three prior acts of terrorism. Through all of the telephone calls the passengers had made and received while on-board the plane, they knew about the fate of the Twin Towers and the Pentagon. In this knowledge, they made the ultimate decision to intercede on behalf of others. They were determined to alter the outcome of their flight and of history.

In their heroic decision to take back control of the plane, they sacrificed themselves as a means of eliminating the hijackers' ability to cause any further damage. The passengers and crew had served the greater good of humanity. In the eyes of God, they had committed the ultimate sacrifice in service of their fellow man. They had laid down their lives in protection of others. I believe this was the reason why the angels had appeared on the field. The angels arrived in honor of the brave men and women on the plane and to transport their souls to God's Heavenly realm. They had come to their earthly domain to once again assist as the lines were drawn between good and evil. Just as the Saints had arisen from their graves after the crucifixion of Jesus, the angels had appeared to escort the souls of God's faithful departed servants aboard Flight 93. The angels had done so to pay homage to the passengers and crew members and revel in the glory of the meaning of their death. Their selfless act of heroism had redeemed our lives and improved the overall well-being of mankind.

CHAPTER 16

THE DARK NIGHT OF THE SOUL

ALL MY LIFE I HAVE HAD THE Grace of God with me. When I was young, I did not comprehend that magnitude of the concept of His grace. I just thought that I was lucky in some way. On occasion, I was blessed by the presence of the Archangel Michael and no matter the life's issue or negative circumstance I faced, it was always resolved for me by some Divine intervention. I heard that familiar voice whisper in my right ear how to handle the situation or to advise of some danger which lay ahead. It took time for me to truly gain the knowledge that God would provide. This understanding moved itself into the light of wisdom. It is a wonderful wisdom to know we are watched over by our guardian angels. Each of us has a direct line of communication to our guardians. They are with us constantly to guide to protect and to heal. We need only to tap into their presence.

During some of the most trying moments of my tenure as a police officer, I learned this truth. I now fully comprehend the magnitude of my guardian angels presence in my life and ability to respond in a time of great danger. I recall an incident in 1992 during the events of the riots in Los Angeles. The neighboring community was hit by violence. On the very night of the ending of the Rodney King case and the acquittal of the Los Angeles police officers, a series of violent incidents rocked the small community.

While on patrol, the officers on duty in the tightly knit communities, received a call from the emergency dispatch relating that a couple was trapped inside their vehicle because a group of males had surrounded them and were now plummeting the car with rocks. The couple was terrorized and had contacted the emergency center via their mobile phone. The dispatcher requested assistance from any available officer cruising the general area. Being I was in close proximity to the location of the couple's vehicle, I advised I would respond. Upon arrival, I observed a vehicle in the middle of the roadway that was surrounded by a group of males. The males were rocking it. It was apparent the car contained two persons sitting in the front seat of the vehicle. I contacted dispatch to relay and confirm that there was a problem and requested immediate backup. I then positioned the patrol vehicle in front of the couple's car. At that point, the males turned their attention to me and moved toward the patrol car. All at once, a rock shattered the windshield of my car and I immediately placed the vehicle's gear in reverse and hastily backed down the street. The males gave chase to my car and allowed a brief time period for the couple to drive away from the scene.

As these events transpired, I kept hearing the Sergeant on the radio directing my actions. A short period of time later, we were all redirected to the housing area of the community. The dispatcher had received complaints of gunfire and vandalism. The officers were all directed by the Sergeant in command to contain those who were causing the disturbance. All of the officers on duty in the neighboring communities responded as backup.

When we arrived at the area in question, I recall hearing shots being fired and then observing the street lights go out. It was dark and the sensations I was feeling felt threatening in nature. I remember taking the shotgun out of the car and placing a riot helmet on my head. All of us were already wearing flank jackets underneath our police uniforms. We were then told to move out, to be careful and to be in constant radio communication with each other. I moved in the direction of where I heard the gunfire. It was so dark and hard to detect any traces of movement by others. All at once, I heard a voice whisper in my ear, "Watch out behind you."

I turned just in time to see a man lurking behind me. All of a sudden, another man came from nowhere and knocked the other man to the ground. As both men fell to the asphalt pavement, I heard the one man say to the other, "Oh no, you don't hurt our police officer."

Even in this difficult tumultuous evening, my heart was filled with such warmth upon hearing the words of this dear man. This wonderful savior of the dark night had called me his police officer. I knew then I had served my community well. The other officers arrived and the man was placed under arrest. I thanked my earthly angel for his bravery and gave him a hug.

After we had cleared the incident, I was in the patrol car and the Sergeant pulled up next to me. He wanted to talk about the night's events as we often did following an incident. He asked about my well-being and I about his. He then said, "I'm worried you have become complacent about dangerous situations."

I replied, "What do you mean?"

The Sergeant then said, "When you were calling dispatch to report your response to the location and the fact that your windshield had just been shattered, you were as calm as if you were ordering a pizza."

I reflected for a moment and smiled. I then related to him, "I was never in danger. My angel is always at my side."

He looked at me in an odd way and just shook his head.

Later that night, I remembered the Sergeant's words and gave thanks to God. For once again he had delivered me from any danger. He had granted me the presence of my guardian angel. Out of this dark and dangerous night, once again came the deliverance of my soul from darkness to light. As I have traveled the days of the rest of my career, these moments of fully knowing that "all will be well regardless" have inspired me to continue through the murkiest waters of my life. I have dredged through the sludge and have wiped my soul clean to enter the light.

A few days later, I had the occasion to once again see the man who had rescued me from danger. I gave him a hug and reiterated to him my gratitude. He responded to me by saying, "You are the only police officer who stops in the community and talks to all of us. You are not just here when there is trouble. You spend time with our children so they get to know you as a person. I appreciate how much you care."

On that disturbing night, there was also great revelation. For on this dark night of the soul, a rebirth had taken place. My faith in others had been restored. And, the event had caused my belief in my guardian angels to be strengthened. I knew without question my celestial protectors were near and whispering in my ear. They were there to guide and protect me just as I was there to do the same for my fellow man.

CHAPTER 17

THE FBI MEETS FEMA

IN EARLY MARCH OF 2008, I HAD the occasion to meet with a representative from the Federal Emergeny Management Agency (FEMA). A mutual friend had arranged the meeting. As a result of an illness, this man was now living in Durango, Colorado. He had moved to Colorado to be in close proximity to a pulmonary clinic in Denver. He related he was now on a medical leave due to a worker's compensation case. He was suffering from a lung ailment that was directly linked to the white powder which had resulted from the fall of the Twin Towers in New York City. His illness had apparently manifested as a result of his prolonged stay and exposure at the Ground Zero crash site.

In my need to know additional information about his illness, he related there were now some 70,000 registered victims of the white powder symptoms. It is a condition which had become prevalent among the first responders and residents of New York City in the following months and years post 9-11. The illness had swept across the City and affected many, just as the dust had done so following the fall of the mighty Twin Towers on that September morning.

When I first met this man, I extended my hand as he did to say hello. His grip was strong against mine. But, as I looked into his eyes, I immediately recognized the pain that I had seen so often in my own. In his lovely green eyes, there peered a mirror of sadness interlocked with a knowledge that life had changed. It had changed so very dramatically in the almost seven years past.

We spent the next couple of hours talking about the events of 9-11, his illness and the resulting PTSD that he was suffering from. He told me about Ground Zero and the initial impact on him. He had spent so much time there. I recall relating to him that I was almost embarrassed to tell him my story after listening to his. When I said these words to him, he looked at me in a very stern manner and said,

"You too have been injured. If what you saw at the site injured your heart and your mind then you too are one of the walking wounded. There is no standard as to who was hurt more."

With these words, my tears began to flow and I unloaded on him. I told him the entire story and included the angels. I queried him for a response. He related he too had felt a presence at Ground Zero. He believed that the forces of good were present as the responders and recovery workers lifted body after body and human remains from the site. He felt an unknown force present as they were bringing out the victims' bodies one at a time. For a brief moment as he spoke, I thought I saw his eyes well up with tears. In that knowledge of his tear about to fall, I believed him to be a kindred spirit. He was indeed a fellow human being that shared the awareness and knowledge of a possible life beyond this earthly domain. I left his presence hoping that someday soon I would have the opportunity to meet with him and talk once again. I also prayed for a miracle to restore his health to him.

To date, I'm not sure if this man will ever fully comprehend the magnitude of the gift he gave me that afternoon during our talk. In his willingness to share his story and listen to mine, he gave me a release. Not only from the concept of sharing in each other's pain, but in the fact that as a man he was willing to admit he too had been affected by the events of 9-11. He had suffered tremendously at Ground Zero. He had experienced great pain and had kept his secret quiet for all too long of a time. He also shared with me he had a "saving grace" in his life. One of his co-workers and friend had extended his hand and helped lift him out of the hole.

At that moment, I was truly in awe of this man. His revelation and his storytelling had allowed me to free myself. I was provided an outlet to unburden my belief I had somehow faltered just because I was a woman. It released me from my prison in my mind. In that moment of recognition, he had saved me from my descent. It was a fall into an oblivion he could well comprehend.

In his reliving of his moments at Ground Zero, I recognized he also had the knowledge of the great black abyss. He understood because he too had peered into the dark hole which I stared at in my own mind. He knew the descent was slow, as would be the recovery. My heart cried out to his spirit, for I knew I was luckier than he. This wonderful man who had served his country when called upon to do so, also bore the knowledge he may soon die. Some of his doctors had indicated he may only live for a few more years. Even with his awareness of "death lurking around the next corner," he was able to share and give comfort to a woman with a broken heart and one whom he barely knew. I am grateful to my fellow patriot and praise him for his mentorship of me. I pray for his recovery and a long life with many years of happiness ahead.

CHAPTER 18

A VOICE IN THE WILDERNESS

ONE MORNING IN EARLY MAY OF 2008, I was very upset with myself. I had been pondering my decision to separate myself from employment with the FBI. I was having a rough time trying to determine which road to take. Should I speak out and tell the world about God's field of angels? Should I continue on with my "call to service" and continue to risk my health. Should I put a request in to the Pittsburgh Division Management for a medical leave (as my physician's had recommended)? Should I just take an early retirement and find other gainful employment? Or, as the woman at FBI Headquarters reminded me, you are not retiring from this job. You in fact are "severing your employment" with the FBI. A harsh term indeed.

How do you sever a 25 year career? It felt as if I were severing a limb from my body or about to lose my brain function. I wondered if I would become as lifeless as a severed limb. Would I just hang there unable to reach for the next opportunity? Would I be incapable of any future success? With all of these thoughts processing in my mind, I was still no further ahead of making a decision. So, as in past times of trouble, I called to God and asked him to give me a sign. I wanted Him to guide me in which of these directions I should go.

As I drove to the office, I whispered a prayer to God. I wanted a clear sign that would give me a definitive answer as to what direction I was to follow. On this particular morning, I was scheduled to assist in co-coordinating an annual "Tension Task Force" meeting with the Pennsylvania Human Relations Commission (PHRC). The meeting was going to be conducted in the Pittsburgh Field Office. This annual meeting provided an opportunity to convene representatives from a diverse group of agencies who were tasked to address civil rights issues. These agencies had been meeting for approximately ten years and were convened post a series of tragic events in the Greater Pittsburgh area. The meeting ran its usual course. There was a great deal of discussion regarding the racial tensions in the schools. There were many comments about the current elections playing a significant part in youth behavioral patterns. There had been an awful lot of conjecture and very little resolution. As in the past, when a meeting was becoming all too bureaucratic in nature, I spoke up. I related to the entire group we were missing an important issue. We were not here to boast about how wonderful we were or the agency that employed us. We were here to discuss matters that would serve "in the best interest of our children."

As I finished my "soap box" oratory about the group getting back on task, the Regional Director for the PHRC requested that I join him at the podium. I complied with his request and hesitantly walked toward him. As I did so, I noticed he was taking a plaque from underneath the podium. I questioned him. He smiled and said, "We have an award for you. This award is the first of its kind. It was created just for you. You have been the voice to be reckoned with. You have said the words that needed to be expressed. You have worked tirelessly to get the job done and succeeded in coordinating an army of agencies."

He then said, "The award is entitled; A Voice in the Wilderness."

I was shocked at his words. I turned to him and he placed the award in my reluctant hands. I then responded, "Is this a nice way of saying that I have a big mouth?"

At my words, the room filled with laughter and humorous comments. I looked around at all of the familiar faces and I smiled. How lucky I felt to be in the midst of such wonderful and dedicated individuals. Each of these lovely creatures was a rare gem in this tumultuous society. I thanked the PHRC for the honor of the award and for the privilege of working with each of the meeting's attendees. I accepted the award on behalf of all of the wonderful agency representatives who had collaborated with all of the endeavors and had worked alongside of me.

In that moment of thanksgiving, it occurred to me I had received my sign. I had been given another gift. I had not only been graced by the award, but also by a sign from above. God had given me the guidance I so desired. A "voice in the wilderness" had taken on two meanings. The language on the award plaque not only expressed thoughts about a job well done. It was also a sign the time had arrived for me to tell the world. It was time to share the story. For it was in the wilderness of that stark landfill I had heard the cry of the lone hawk. The hawk had announced the presence of the angels and the reminder that the spirit of God was all around us. He was there in that moment of crisis when the world cried to Him for help. It was a story which needed a strong voice in order to be heard. I had heard the cry in the wilderness and had visited a great wasteland which was once my mind and my soul. It had now been filled with the knowledge of my future purpose. In the middle of that field of devastation on 9-11, I had heard a voice in the wilderness. It was a voice which had called me to reach higher and respond to God's call to service.

CHAPTER 19

SUPERWOMAN HAS LEFT THE ROOM

BETWEEN JUNE OF 2005 AND APRIL OF 2008, I spent many months participating in therapy sessions. I did so willingly but only half believing I was suffering from an illness. At this time, I had limited my awareness and knowledge of truly understanding the meaning of Post Traumatic Stress Disorder (PTSD) or the resulting factors on my health. My inability to truly grasp the concept of the illness made it increasingly harder to accept the diagnosis. On one of my first visits to a new psychotherapist, I had the opportunity to discuss with the Doctor the definition of PTSD. She gently queried if any of my treating medical professionals had shared the clinical definition of the illness. I explained no one had given me the information. She then inquired if I would care to read from the medical book that provided the "official terminology" used to describe and diagnose the illness to insurance providers. I indicated that being a visual learner it might be helpful to read the information. So, she handed me the little red book which was opened at a particular page and I began to read from it. As I read the definition with all of its symptoms, I queried as to how many of the symptoms were necessary to indicate the illness was present in a patient. She related that two or more symptoms needed to be present. I then began to laugh out loud. The Doctor was surprised at my response and asked about it. I related I was just laughing at the fact that I had all of the symptoms except for two.

I then began to cry and said, "For the rest of my life, I am now going to be labeled as a psychiatric patient."

The psychologist responded, "Yes, by some you will be. However, medical professionals will relate to you it is the only psychiatric illness which requires a traumatic injury in order to begin. PTSD is the result of a traumatic event which then led to your illness and a decline in your health."

I was not very comforted by her words. I knew all to well what the label would mean in my profession. There would be no sympathy from my fellow law enforcement officers for the term PTSD. I would be perceived as the woman who "went over the edge." I feared I would lose my credibility and become the woman who couldn't take the pressure of the job. It would be just like my first months as a police officer when the men repeatedly taunted me about being female. I had heard all too many times the repetition of how a woman did not belong in policing. We were the weaker sex and incapable of doing the job. I had become engaged in all too many arguments in those early years. Now, as I pondered those conversations and disputes, I realized women did belong in this world of law enforcement. However, as a woman, it was necessary to somehow retain the identity and essence of a female. It had been a particularly hard task for me to retain my personality of long ago. It required me to have two distinct personas. The one was obvious to most people who I was acquainted with and the other was only apparent to those who truly knew me and cared for my well-being.

In the latter days of my career, I had often said to the men, "I came into this profession a nice girl and I'm leaving it as a woman I hardly recognize."

This was the harsh reality of my almost 25 years in the profession. On this particular moment of understanding, I realized "Superwoman had finally learned her lesson and had now left the room."

Her leaving made me feel a sense of great loss and sadness. How humbling those first moments of recognition were. In order to heal, I would have to shed "my persona" and retrieve the remnants of the soft woman from days gone by.

Superwoman had been my identity for so long and I had worn her uniform with pride. My ego, my fidelity, my integrity and my bravery were all interwoven into her cape. Yet I had also worn it to shield myself from the world. Every piece of material and each thread that created the red, white and blue patchwork of my cape had intertwined into it some aspect of my personality. Nestled underneath that cape lay the essence of a wounded female who had somehow given up on her life. I was still capable and functional with my work. I knew very well the meaning of "over-achieving." But, just like an alcoholic, I had been in denial all too long. And when it came to my personal life, I had become immobilized by fear and my efforts to move forward. I had lost the desire to reach out to the new. My inability to let go of the past overburdened my heart and my mind. So, on this day of recognition, I was humbled. I realized the magnitude of my ego. Now, as I removed my symbolic uniform and cape, my old persona of Lillie was requested to return. I hoped somewhere deep inside me the Lillie of long ago was present and waiting to reemerge. I wondered had she survived and just how much of her had remained intact. I was hopeful through the various therapies I was about to undertake, she would feel free to come back to life and become a shining beacon of light as I moved through the phases of healing.

In those first few glimpses of self-recognition and admission of my fear, I saw pieces of my puzzled self as I used to be. It left me with a realization that I had a decision to make. Did I really want to live or did I want to die?

If I chose life, there lay a hard road ahead. The days would be filled with doctor appointments, medications, possible loss of my job, my income, shame, pain, sorrow, regret and alienation from those I have loved and worked so closely with. I would be leaving behind my comrades in arms. Or more to the point, they would trail away from me. Then, there was my family and friends. How would they react? Would they be willing to support me in my time of need?

If I chose death, all I need to do is give in to the pain within and let my mind and body wear away with neglect and time. With my current state of health it would be an easier road to travel. As I looked in the mirror for any glimmer of an answer, I heard a voice say to me, "Live, prosper and succeed."

As I listened to the strong yet soft tone of the voice, I recognized it to be that of my Father. I felt the tears well up and the emotion rise from the pit of my soul and surge to the opening of my throat. Then, I heard my own voice cry out, "Elohim, Elohim, Elohim, please rescue me from this wasteland and restore me to my destiny. I can not do this on my own."

In my moment of requiem, a stirring in my soul rose from the pit of my being and I was moved to my redemption and the light. What I thought would be my "swan song" had become my "aria" of saving grace.

CHAPTER 20

A SECRET REVEALED

ON SEPTEMBER 11, 2007, I HAD BEEN invited to serve as a guest speaker for the annual anniversary mass of the 9-11 service held at St. Thomas More University Parish church in Indiana, Pennsylvania. I had received the invitation from a man who shared a mutual friendship with a colleague of mine who served with the Pennsylvania Emergency Management Agency. Although I had agreed to speak, I was very hesitant to do so at the time. My mind kept contemplating the possibility of revealing the entire story in front of a congregation of people who I did not know. I pensively spent the days leading up to the presentation teetering between my thoughts of what was appropriate in the delivery of the speech. I wondered, was it the right time to share God's message to a group of virtual strangers? Was it a good idea to reveal it in the church setting? Was I not a sinner and still tainted with the sins of my thoughts and deeds? Did I dare speak and possibly be rebuked?

As the day swiftly approached, I contacted an old friend who also happened to be a publicist. She and I had been friends since our days in junior high school. We were acquainted with each other for almost 40 years. And, although we had very little contact with each other over the past twenty odd years, upon any re-contact we had always picked up with our relationship as if no time had passed. She had also secured a place in my heart for being one of the true friends in my life. She was one of the few people from my past that had supported me and did not abandon me when I became pregnant at an early age in life. She stood by my side and helped me stay strong in my convictions about the situation. We had a great deal in common for our personalities were similar in design. We also shared an amusing story about my wedding day that we laughed about each and every time we meet.

It was on the date of my nuptial vows that I very much became aware of her fortitude. Even in her youth, she had strength of spirit that shined through to the outside of her being. During the wedding reception, all of the guests were seated around the festive tables and dinner had just been served to some three hundred individuals. All were quietly eating their food when the main doors swung open to the reception hall. As the doors slammed against the wall, the sound caused all eyes to move in the direction of the noise and standing there, in the entrance to the hall, stood my friend in all of her glory and embarrassment. As she realized that all eyes were now upon her, she attempted to back out of the door. All at once, I caught her eye and I gestured for her to come see me up on the stage. For, it was a typical Italian style wedding with the bride, the groom, the wedding party and the parents proudly displayed above the guests on the stage for all eyes to gaze upon. With great hesitation, my friend approached and as she climbed the few stairs to where I sat, all eyes were watching. When she finally made her way to me, we embraced and laughed. She then said, "Now, I know how Moses felt when he parted the Red Sea. I just parted the great White Sea and it was pretty scary."

When she finished uttering her words, it took me but a minute to realize what exactly she had meant because, as I looked out at all of the faces of the guests, she was the only African American in the room. As we continued to laugh, the others at the head table heard her comments and soon the laughter was contagious. As each of the members of the bridal party caught her meaning, they shared in her amusement. At that time in my life, it was one of those rare moments that I realized there was still an ability to laugh my way through an uncomfortable scenario of events. It was also very clear to me that I admired my friend's tenacity. Under an extreme moment of discomfort, she had prevailed through her gift of levity. No wonder she had chosen a profession as a publicist. Even at her youthful age, she proved that she could handle herself in any situation and, in that instance, quite well. I guess that this was the reason that I chose to once again reach out to her for help. A long time ago, when my heart was stilled by fear of moving forward in my life, she stood up on a stage and brought comfort to my life. She had managed to turn an awkward situation into a joyful moment of memory. I hoped that this friend would bring her own kind of magic to the present moment as well. I was in dire need of her comfort and help. I needed her to make me smile again during a very stressful moment in the present time just like she had done so many years ago.

As we spoke on the telephone days leading up to the pending speech, I related to her the events of 9-11. After telling her about the field of angels, I spent a few minutes explaining my present dilemma about the upcoming presentation. I asked her for any professional advice that she could render. She offered to me a plenary of suggestions that made sense and also offered to travel with me to the church and provide support to me as well. I was elated to know she would be traveling with me, for I not only needed her professional guidance, but her friendship too. It would also give us some time to further discuss the issue and she could play "devil's advocate" for me while I drove. When the evening of the presentation arrived, my friend and I drove to the church with great trepidation. It was an unnerving 90 minutes that we traveled. The anniversary date of 9-11 had always made me feel anxious and on this particular one I was filled with a high level of anxiety. All too soon, we arrived at the church and as I drove through the parking lot, I realized that the lot was at full capacity. At that moment, I became very apprehensive at the aspect of speaking because based on the number of cars parked in the lot, there were going to be many more people sitting in the pews than I had first imagined.

As we walked into the church, my eyes gazed across the many pews now filled with people. I hesitated at the door and my friend put her hand on my shoulder and gently guided me into the vestibule. Her gentle touch gave me some comfort and before too long I regained some composure. Within a moment's time, we were greeted by the gentleman who had extended the invitation to me. We spoke for a brief moment and soon we were whisked away to be introduced to the parish priest. As I spoke to the priest about my intended presentation, I felt a quiet calming take hold of me. I again pondered the aspect of revealing the entire story to the congregation of people eagerly awaiting the start of the annual service. I provided a brief description of the events of 9-11, the angel visitation and asked him to help me decide what to do. As I finished describing my story and concerns, the priest placed his hand on my shoulder and explained I didn't need his guidance for God had already guided me to the church and it was quite possible I was there to share my story as a means of promoting some healing for me and for others as well. It was then I felt a huge burden lift from my soul. I had indeed arrived at this very destination by God's design. Was it the moment to begin some type of healing? Was it the moment of revelation? If indeed it was, what did I fear? Was it not God's story and that of His angels? All of these questions flashed through my mind as I tried to draw courage from my spirit.

Within minutes, we strolled into the church. At that moment, I noticed all of the men were dressed in their Knights of Columbus regalia. I was very familiar with this distinctive clothing because my own Father had been a member of this prestigious corps of men. As I peered at the faces of these men, my mind slipped back to a moment in time and the picture of my Dad lying in his coffin and wearing his Knights of Columbus uniform. He had been laid to rest wearing his black tuxedo, crisply ironed white shirt, red sash and his cherished saber. The memory of Dad and his affection for the association had quieted the restlessness in me and a peace had entered my soul. In that moment of memory, I felt a calming energy take hold. And, I was awakened to the concept that telling the truth about that fateful day of 9-11 may initiate my healing. I instinctively knew it was time to release the story. If for no other reason than to honor my Dad and the men in the room who had shared his vocation as a member of the royal knights of the church.

As my time to speak drew near, I rose to my feet and slowly walked to the altar. Before I could give it any thought, the words began to exit my mouth, they began to flow with such ease. The motion of the room slowed down and my mind resurrected the visions of the Shanksville field. With each new phrase that I uttered, my mind cleared and the ropes that had bound my heart for so long began to untangle their hold upon my emotions. I felt an indescribable feeling coming from the recesses of my soul and I stilled the urge to scream an alleluia. As I contemplated all that I wanted to say, the tears began to fall from my eyes. It was then I looked to my friend and she was crying too.

In an instant, I moved to leave that altar and as I did the entire congregation rose to their feet and the room errupted into a standing ovation. In that moment of time, my mind took note of the real reason for the congregation's reaction. It was in praise of God and His divine sign of grace. It was for the angels that had arrived at the field to recover the brave souls. And most especially, it was to recognize the heroic deeds of the brave men and women who had perished on board Flight 93. As I walked off the altar and back to my seat, I felt a deep stirring of pride enter into my being. I had completed a task that I thought was impossible for me. In this beautiful and simply decorated church, in front of a group of people I did not know, I had shared the story that had lay dormant for so long inside of me. I had feared a negative reaction but, instead, had received recognition for being stoic enough to stand on my conviction that the story of the field of angels was indeed true.

Before I left the church that night, many of the congregation took the time to relate to me a story about their own encounters with angels. As I listened to the different stories, I reflected upon the many blessings in all of our lives. In the most trying moments, many of us are fortunate enough to be visited and touched by an angel. The angels serve as our guides and protectors. And on this night, I had entered the church fearful of the unknown and once again had received the visitation of the angels. However, this time it was not the winged celestial visitors I had witnessed, but, the many kind and caring people of the parish. I left the church with a sense of courage and a new direction. In the words of the revelation I had spoken, I had unleashed a whole new set of angels and had been granted the gift of comfort from the many who were sitting ever so patiently in the pews. In their need to listen and hear, I had been restored with a new sense of purpose and hope of the life yet ahead.

Later that evening, as I left the church, I was given two lovely gifts. The parish priest gave me a cross that he had carried with him from Jerusalem. As I touched the cross, a warm feeling was emitted into my hand. The cross, a most sacred article in the Christian faith, was also one that had been brought from the holiest of locations in the Middle East. It was an excellent reminder of my faith and the suffering that Jesus had endured in order to provide resurrection to us all. It reminded me that the strength of conviction of one's faith is the very backbone of one's soul. As I held the cross admiringly in my hand, a wonderful female parishioner also bestowed me with a prayer shawl she had knitted herself. I was moved by the precious gift received because when she placed the delicately knitted shawl in my hands, my heart rippled through to the very core of my emotions and my battered mind exhaled. The cross now hangs on the wall of my grandchildren's playroom. There it gives watch over the children as they play, ever mindful of God's grace and light. The shawl lies inside my bedroom dresser drawer and on occasion I retrieve it from its hiding place. As I unwrap the lovely little shawl and place it on my shoulders it is a reminder to me of God's protection and it helps alleviate my fears and serves as my shield of armor.

The memory of that evening in the church burns brightly in my mind and will remain forever more. As I close my eyes, the vision of all the parishioners and the handsome men of the Knights of Columbus as they stood brilliantly dressed in their noblemen's robes sits firmly in view. The lovely group of men stood tall in their loyalty to the church and they were a symbolic reminder of the strong and sturdy structure of the congregation's faith that obviously sustains their lives. The memory of their presence burns in my heart to the moment in time when my Dad lay inside his casket. And there, standing next to him, were his fellow knights. As each person walked to view my Dad's remains, his colleagues stood guard to illuminate their path and his journey to the golden gates above. They were there to remind Dad that even in death he was not left without his comrades in arms. It was a reminder to all present we are never alone.

CHAPTER 21

A LILY IN BLOOM

OVER THE NEXT FEW MONTHS AS I entered through my initial journey to heal, I experienced a myriad of emotions and physical pain. The physical symptoms seemed to exasperate in every direction. On occasion, I would become fearful because an area of my body would experience a new pain pattern. One of the most confusing of the emotions that had now entered my thoughts was a sense of lost confidence. This sensation was so new to my psyche. Because over the last years in my profession, I had acquired a strong sense of self and ability to address most any situation that would arise on a both personal and professional level. But, in recent months, my sense of self-confidence dissipated with each visit to the doctor and each discussion which related to my mental health. The more often I thought about the situation, the deeper I fell into a state of anxiety and self loss.

In August of 2008, I once again received a gift that assisted my healing and restoration of self-confidence. I was in a rush to make a physical therapy appointment. The morning had been very hectic. A friend had been visiting my home and he needed a ride to his truck. I was already running late. I made an attempt to reschedule my appointment for a later hour that day.

However, the receptionist at the therapist's office informed me that there were no other available time slots for this particular day. So, I hurried to take my friend to his destination and to make my therapy appointment.

As I was traveling on Route 56 near my home, I approached an intersection and noticed that the traffic light had turned red. I started to take my foot off of the gas pedal and slow down. I then noticed that a dark-colored SUV vehicle traveling about 50 to 60 feet ahead of me because it did not appear to be slowing its pace. On the contrary, the car seemed to be traveling at a high rate of speed with no apparent signs of the driver activating the brake lights.

All at once, the SUV drove straight through the intersection and struck a truck. The truck stopped on impact and the SUV swerved slightly to the left. I immediately drove to the vicinity of the vehicles and parked my car on the side of the road. I exited my car and ran to the truck first. Inside the truck sat two men, both of whom appeared to be alright and were on their cell phones. I asked about their well being and if they had called 911. I recognized one of the men as an old family friend. Both of them indicated that they were fine and that the police had been notified. I then moved to the SUV and noticed that there was a great deal of smoke coming from the vehicle. As I moved to look inside the SUV, I heard a woman screaming that her car was on fire. I told her that I was there to help and she should calm down and turn off the ignition. I asked if she was injured and noticed that there was also a small boy sitting in a safety seat in the rear of the vehicle.

I opened the rear door of the SUV and asked the little boy, "Are you hurt?"

The little boy responded, "No, I'm not hurt but, I'm scared."

I quickly said to him, "I'm scared too. But, we need to get you and your Mom out of the car."

I then asked him if he would allow me to help him out of the car. He shook his head and said, "Yes."

I did a quick pat down of the child to make sure that there were no apparent injuries and advised the woman that I was going to remove her son from the vehicle. She gave me permission to do so and I gently lifted the boy from his safety seat. As I was lifting him, the woman again began to scream that her vehicle was on fire. I quickly reacted and told her to immediately move to the rear of the vehicle and climb out of the back doors. I explained that both of the front doors were damaged and could not be opened. I then carried her son to the side of the road. At that point, several other persons had arrived on the scene. The woman soon followed behind us. As I carried the boy to a safe place, I noticed that there were chemicals spilling from the SUV onto the roadway.

It was only a few minutes later that the police officers arrived at the scene and took charge of the situation. I recognized one of the officers and he inquired if I had been involved in the accident. I explained that I had witnessed the incident. I then gave the police officers my version of the accident and left to go to my therapy appointment.

In the immediate moments following the vehicle accident, I heard that familiar voice inside my ear. The voice indicated that I had received three gifts on this day. The three gifts were as follows. The first, God is indeed in control of the dominoes in my life. All of us live in His design. A few minutes earlier or a few minutes later and I would not have been at the accident scene. On this day, the dominoes were lined up for me to be at that particular place and at that exact time. It was a reminder that God had supreme control of my destiny.

The second gift was the doctors had indeed been right about the pattern the PTSD would take when I would be required to respond to a new traumatic event. My doctors had advised me that in the event of any trouble, because of prior conditioning, my body would instantly release endorphins. For almost immediately, I felt a sense of euphoria running through my body. My adrenalin pumped and the endorphins surged through my veins. I felt wonderful and relaxed. This feeling of relaxation was the direct opposite of the anxiety I had felt for the past years.

The third gift was the momentary return of my self confidence. Over the past year, with my health problems, the diagnosis of PTSD, compounded by the isolation from my job, I had lost some of my confidence. I had felt less than whole. But, in those first moments following the crash, I was capable of responding in an appropriate manner. My training kicked into high gear and it was once again showtime. I hadn't lost my ability to serve my fellow men. I was still capable of helping someone in need. I was still a viable human being and valuable to our society. My confidence in myself was indeed restored.

On this day, despite the morning trauma of the vehicle accident, I had been given three new gifts. I drove away from the scene feeling much better about myself and my life. It truly was a blessed day. Not only did God save four people from any major injuries, He also restored my sense of self worth.

Three days later, one of my prized Calla Lilies bloomed. The Lily bloomed to its vibrant flame color. The deep lemon yellow of the blossom tipped with the red edges stood tall against the green plume of its leaves. The Lily had not bloomed for three years. In my mind, it was a symbolic gesture of the dominoes again falling into place. I viewed the Calla Lily blooming as a sign of new life about to begin. It was the beginning not only for my prized plant, but for me as well.

CHAPTER 22

RECONCILIATION OF MY MIND AND SOUL

IT HAS NOW BEEN TEN YEARS SINCE 9-11. It has taken me this long to determine the appropriate time to share my story of God's field of angels. I do so now as a means of self healing and reflection, for the greater good of His people and in an attempt to move forward with my life. For these past few years, I felt as if my heart and mind were frozen in time. I have felt like a barren frozen wasteland unable to feel the warmth of the sun or the compassion of my heart. I have kept reliving those brief moments on that field in Shanksville when the angels first appeared and provided some hope to all of us who suffered that September day. Although others have experienced greater suffering than I as a result of 9-11, I too have suffered many stressful days. I have continuously worried over the aspect of relating my tale to all those willing to listen and read. I have hidden my story in the quiet recesses of my mind and heart. I have spoken of my story to only several trusted friends, colleagues and medical professionals. And, on September 11, 2007, I shared my story with a congregation of strangers at a Catholic Church located in Indiana, Pennsylvania. All who have heard it have also indicated my story must be told to all who are willing to listen, interpret and believe.

So, I share this story of the "field of angels" with mixed emotion. One side of me contains great joy at the prospect of sharing it with others who will believe. The other side of me is very hesitant. I hold my breath awaiting the reaction of those people who are so important to me. There is my family who already believes me to be slightly strange. There are my colleagues that I served with and somehow never quite fit in with. I wonder will they believe in what I witnessed. Will they question my sanity?

At this point in my life, I am sure of only one thing as it relates to my story. It is time for others to know there are angels walking this Earth. They wait in readiness to serve and protect. Angels are the kindred spirits of all of us in law enforcement and those of us who rise to the occasion as momentary heroes in response to life's terrible tragedies. They are guardians standing ready to protect us and defend us from harm. They are guides prepared to escort us on our journeys. They are healers ready to slay the most heinous of diseases. And, if we are fortunate, at the end of our lives, the angels carry us back to the loving arms of God when He finally calls us home. The angels serve us and hear us when we cry to the Heavens for help. Just like that fall day of September 11, 2001, when the legion of Angels carried the souls of our fallen heroes of Flight 93.

I can only pray this story gives hope to those in despair, and those who still anguish over their losses and sorrows in their life. I have been blessed with "amazing grace" and now wish to share it with others in need of it. God is here. If we open our hearts and allow Him into our lives, He shares His love in the most obscure moments. In our most troubling times when we cry to Him for help, He sends the warmth of His heart to us. God sends us His Guardian Angels to serve, protect, guide and heal.

The loneliness and isolation have been the hardest part of these past nine years. In order to sustain the demeanor I needed to continue on my path of self-protection, I kept myself from truly feeling or expressing my pain. I abandoned my need to extend myself to others. I denied myself many an opportunity to reach out for help. I limited myself the ability to "peek around the corner" and express my feelings to only a select few immediate family members and close friends. Every choice I made, I did so only after over-analyzing the relevance of the situation. I had to retain the ability to control my feelings and thoughts in order to control the outcomes. I had to control all aspects of my life. I had to control my femininity and those natural instincts that made me a woman. I had to abandon all of my female intuition in order to survive. It was a role reversal. My naturally friendly demeanor turned into a guarded and paranoid human being.

However, it was in the absolution of myself that the true essence of my healing began. The pain and the stress came from my inability to forgive myself and the memory of those significant persons from my past that I could not let go of. The negative situations had faded but the faces of those that I had wronged and who had wronged me remained buried deep inside my soul. They had all accumulated over the years. My karma had developed and manifested into the illnesses that now plagued my body. I not only had the physical pain with the many symptomatic responses, but my mind would not absolve my soul. My soul wailed inside and pleaded for my mind to "let go."

It was only in the final stages of "digging in" to recognize the buried pain that the absolution and self-restoration began. I had to shovel through all of the layers of the mud that had buried the real me. My life had been stilled and dormant, unable to open to the light. In the letting go of the pain, lay the return to the path of light. As I learned to "just breathe", the layers of mud began to slowly dissolve. The murky waters that were once present began to clear. My self cleansing was apparent. I now allowed myself to feel the pain. The pain provided me the outlet to regain my voice. It was a voice that echoed and shared the stories of my past. My voice then began to resonate to my soul and it lifted in rejoice.

My journey of spirituality began on that fateful day of 9-11. It continues with the release of my story and with the healing of my heart, my mind, my body and my soul. For it is only in the release of my story, that I believe emotional and physical healing will begin. In the holding of my story, I became sick with fatigue and anxiety. I have held my story tight to my bosom like a protective mother ready to fight off any threat to her child. I have guarded it and myself for all too long of a time. But now, I understand the true essence of healing will only come with the release and the "letting go". In order to heal and move forward, I must first dive into the recesses of my thoughts and feelings. I must allow myself to first feel the remnants of the old in order to allow for the new. So, I now take my proverbial leap off of the cliff and pray that the net will appear.

CHAPTER 23

WEEDING THROUGH

AS I MOVED THROUGH THE VARIOUS STAGES of the healing process, I would periodically use the "Archangel Oracle" cards that I had purchased during a visit to a health spa. The beautifully designed cards are part of collection that were developed by Doreen Virtue, a renowned psychologist and author who works very closely with the angelic realm in her healing practice. The cards became a form of release for me in my journey and repeated attempts to heal. Almost each time that I read from the cards, the Archangel Jophiel card would be pulled from the deck. It was the card that was inscribed with the words "Clear Your Space." The lovely decorated card with the alluring features of the Archangel gives notice to the reader to "Get rid of the clutter, clear the energy around you." Each time I would hold the card in my hand, I would ponder, what clutter? How many more closets, cupboards, dresser drawers and storage boxes were in need of my rummaging through? There were not many spaces left in my small home that I had not ripped apart over the past few months. But, as I would again and again pull the same card from the pile, I was reminded that the Archangels were more knowledgeable than I about the subject and were obviously trying to get my attention regarding some type of clutter that I had not yet addressed.

As I continued to rummage through the various holding places of my home, my belongings and the mementos of my life, I finally realized the message that the Archangel was trying to deliver. It had nothing to do with my physical space and everything to do with the cluttered space around my heart and my mind. Both of these vital parts of my body were clogged with the innumerable memories that lay buried inside of them. As I became keenly aware of the true meaning of the card, I realized that my heart and mind had been filled to the brink like one of those portable, on-demand storage containers. And inside the locked container of my heart and mind, lay the remnants of the past.

The importance of looking at the memories of those passing days was now apparent to me. It was necessary to do so before the present time would make any sense and the future would have a chance to manifest. So as I peeled open the many compartments to my mind, I peered into those events in my life that had clogged the process of healing. Each new space that I visited revealed an element of surprise about the past memories of 9-11. Memories that had remained dormant in the dark places of my mind and the hidden spaces of my heart. If I was to truly heal, I would need to look at the musty corners in order for the clear fresh air to fill the dusty hollows of my space.

It was in this moment of clarity, I knew I had to begin to slowly weed through the clutter and start with the very beginning of that September day. I had to inch my way to the place where all of the debris began to build. I had to take hold of that place in order to ultimately take back my life.

I needed to understand why I continued to hoard all of the memories and why I allowed them to remain. If indeed I intended to heal from the trauma, it was necessary to determine where had I become frozen with fear. It was time to weed through all those leftover memories that remained ingrained inside of my psyche and finally let go of the past events. If I could accomplish this task, maybe it would be possible to eradicate the leftover rubbish that needed discarded. And, perhaps, if I could successfully clear my space, there would be room for spiritual growth.

CHAPTER 24

THE SOUTHWEST TRAIL

IN OCTOBER OF 2007, I MADE A trip to Durango, Colorado to visit the significant man in my life. On this trip, I not only traveled to Durango, but to other areas of the Southwest as well. As I ventured to each new location, I experienced a great awareness of the vastness of the mountain ranges. I became keenly familiar with the sensation and movement of energy. Each of the ranges were varied not only in size, shape, coloration and contour, but contained different vortexes of energy. Some of the energy was very subtle and soothing. It moved so lightly and mixed ever so gently with the wind. Some of the energy was heavy and swirled with the movement of air. I could actually sense the density of it as it pressed against my skin. I could feel it with each breath through my nostrils. No matter the variance of energy, I could feel it as it moved across and through the recesses of my body. I constantly felt invigorated and alive. My senses were keen. My hope was everlasting. My desire to communicate and express my emotions became an important part of each day. The clarity of thought moved me in ways I had not yet felt or sensed prior to this experience. Before my trips to the Southwest, I had heard some stories from my friends about the magnificence of the mountains and the energy that they contained. Now, as I traveled through the mountain ranges, across the plains and deserts, I understood their meaning and purpose.

A short time into my return journey back to Durango, I observed what I believed were the forms of angels on the tops of various mountain ranges. They appeared only upon the rugged contours of the mountaintops. Each form stood upon the rough edges of the peaks with its arms extended toward the sky. I saw the forms in a very abstract view and observed hues of lavender and blue around them. At first glance, the form appeared to be human in nature. Yet, it was so obtuse that identifying its true essence was not clearly definable at the time. I knew that this was a sign sent from God in an attempt to relate some meaning to me.

It took about a month for me to realize what the visions of the angels on the mountain ranges had meant. It was a cold Thanksgiving afternoon. The weather was quite gloomy and I was feeling somewhat depressed. My post-traumatic stress was kicking in and once again I worried about the outcome of another episode. As my mood worsened, I knelt down to pray. I began to meditate. I recall asking God for help with the sudden mood change. As I raised my hands to the Heavens, I immediately sensed the answer which eluded me regarding the vision on the mountain peaks. In that instant, the message of the vision had such clarity. It was sheer perfection. It was not merely an angel I had seen. The vision was symbolic of a human being rising to the essence of its higher power. The image of the human was raising its hands to the Heavens calling to God and seeking the universal energy of the mountains. The louder the person's cries increased, the more the universal energy began to move across the sky. As the form moved to outstretch its arms, a metamorphosis took place. From the depths of the Earth, a softness of feathered wings began to develop. The underneath of the arms began to transform into those of angel's wings. The pale blue color of the sky was shrouded by the shimmers and bursts of brilliant blues and purple hues of the celestial form. As the two forms became one, the natural light of the sky intermixed with the radiance and purity of spiritual white light above the extended arms.

At this moment of recognition, it was apparent to me the form was clearly providing the egress to my future path. It was the passage of my destiny. My fear of disclosure had dissipated. My need to hide and not speak the truth was gone. It was now time to open up my mind and heart and allow the world to know of my story about the field of angels on that fateful September day. It was finally time to leap off the ledge and allow the net to appear. I should no longer worry about the outcome of my story telling. For in the disclosure of my story, the integrity of the message would reign supreme. Those who chose to believe would be comforted by the message. They would know the truth of my journey. They would recognize their own story and belief within mine. I could no longer be distraught about any disbelief because that was not my journey. My journey was to provide the testimony of the angels in the field. It was my responsibility to carry God's message to the believers and seekers of His truth. It was my duty to regain my strength of courage and composure in order to deliver His message to those that were willing to hear.

The message of the vision had such clarity and affirmation. This magnificent image was again another gift from God. It would serve as the reminder that as human beings we are constantly evolving toward our higher power. Most of us consistently strive in working at bettering ourselves. After all, is not prayer the heightened words and thoughts of our inner selves? Is not prayer the very purpose and essence of bettering ourselves and asking for help in doing so? The illustration of the human to angel metamorphosis would be the best manner to depict these thoughts and the meaning of the vision. It would be the first symbol of what the book contained. It would serve as an awakening in each of us to respond to the deeper recesses of our souls. It would be the lasting image of God's message in my story. It would best serve as the testimony that good does conquer evil. It is a lasting message of hope, trust and His greatest gift of love for all of His children.

CHAPTER 25

LIFE'S PURPOSE

DOES ANYONE BELIEVE THAT VICTORY CAN BE achieved without facing danger?

This was a quote from the latest version of the movie about "Pearl Harbor."

One evening as I sat contemplating my life's purpose, this quote came to mind and I pondered the relevance of defining and understanding it. I began to recall a series of events that made me think long and hard about the reasons for not only my life but those of the passengers and crew members aboard Flight 93. I questioned, what was my life's purpose and would I be able to fulfill my sacred contract? As I pondered this question about myself, I was very sure of at least two reasons for my existence. I did know first and foremost I was born to be a mother and bring my daughter into this world. She in turn would deliver her three daughters and son to the boundaries of this Earth and serve as a beacon of guiding light on their behalf. This was the most important aspect of my life. But, what else was there to be completed?

I learned in these quiet moments of contemplation to truly identify your life's purpose one must explore the content of their life. I had often asked myself questions regarding this very matter. Had I truly helped others to improve their lives? Had my life had any positive effect on those that I loved? Had I helped others to reach a level of excellence? My Father had so often explained it was important to know you walked the Earth to help others achieve their goals in life. It was of value to become a person of quality and in turn to assist others on their journey as well.

In 1984, in the early stages of my law enforcement career, I found a beautiful little news clip about the life of Benjamin Franklin. In the clip, it highlighted the author's query to Mr. Franklin regarding his apparent wealth and material gain.

Mr. Franklin replied, "It was not a true test of a man's character if he had acquired great wealth or property. It is however a true testimony of one's character if they have been responsible for positively affecting at least one person's life for the better."

When I first read this little ditty, I cut it out and taped it on the inside of my locker in the squad room. Each tour of duty, as I opened my locker, this message was the first thing I would see. I read it each day as a reminder of the message. The message would remind me of my place in the world and as a member of the law enforcement profession. I was there to serve and protect. I was there to help others in a time of need. I was there to give guidance and strength when necessary.

On my first day as a police officer, I experienced an embarrassing moment with my new partner that would become a permanent reflection of the following years while patrolling with him.

After having made repeated attempts to buckle my new gunbelt into place, I lost my redheaded temper and began cursing at it. Without noticing that my Mom had entered my bedroom, she startled me when I finally noticed her standing in the doorway. As I looked up at her, she asked, "Lillie Marie who are you yelling at?"

As I continued to wrestle with the stiff black leather object in my hand, I gruffly responded to her by saying, "I'm angry at this damn gunbelt. I can't get the clasp to fasten."

She looked at me rather intently and replied, "Why don't you get the other officer to help you with the belt?"

I looked up at her in disbelief and said, "Great idea Mom. He can just help dress the incompetent woman and that should make him feel real confident about my abilities to work with him. How could he believe that I could handle policing if I can't even buckle a damn belt?"

On my comment, she said, "You know that I don't like it when you swear."

She mumbled something else that I couldn't quite hear, shrugged her shoulders, and then promptly walked out of the room. Within seconds of her leaving my bedroom, I realized that it was about time for my partner to be arriving to pick me up. So, I hurriedly grabbed the rest of my gear and ran from my room. When I arrived downstairs and opened the front door, to my surprise, there stood my partner already waiting for me. He was talking with both of my parents and my Dad seemed to be rapidly firing a multitude of questions at him. It took everything in me not to remind my Dad that my partner had not arrived at the house to take me on a date, but was there to drive me to work. I stilled the need to express the sarcasm and just said, "Hello."

As I finished my welcome, he looked up at me and smiled and immediately said to me, "Your Mother tells me that you're having a tough time fastening your gunbelt to your pants. Why don't you come over here and let me see if I can help you with it? Don't be embarrassed it has happened to all of us when we first try to adjust it. And, don't worry, I won't tell anybody else that I helped you to get dressed. It will be our secret."

Little did I know at that moment the secret would not be left between us. This scene would be revisited for many years to come. It was shared with all too many a police officer when my partner felt the need to poke fun of the rookie he had helped to groom into a cop.

As he finished his words, he burst into laughter and I felt my face go flush. I glanced over at my Mom who was standing nearby and gave her an angry look. She again shrugged her shoulders and walked inside the house. I hesitantly walked over to him and handed him the gunbelt. With one quick movement of his hands, the belt was snapped into place. As the snugly fit leather piece of equipment fastened around my waist, I looked up at him and thanked him for his assistance. He again just smiled at me and said nothing in return. I was grateful for his silence.

After spending these embarrassing moments with both my Mother and Father, my partner and I began to walk toward the patrol car. At which time, my Dad requested to have a private moment with me and politely asked my partner to wait for me in the patrol car. My Father opened the front door of our home and held the door for me. He then requested I come inside the house for a quiet moment of reflection with him. We entered the kitchen and my Dad asked me to turn to him and look in his eyes. I did as he requested.

He then said, "I'm not sure I agree with your choice of a job. I'm not sure I want one of my daughters working as a police officer. With that said, I want you to know I am proud of you. You have always had the eye of the tiger. However, if you chose to begin today, there are a few rules that go along with this new job. If you are agreeable to these rules, I'll approve of your choice."

I shook my head in agreement and listened to his words that followed.

Dad continued with his litany and said, "These are your rules. First, if you ever start acting like the men and lose your femininity, you have to quit. Never forget to use your God given talents as a woman. If you ever start behaving like the men and swearing, you have to quit the job. Never forget for one minute from where you came and only through the Grace of God and the fact you had good parents did you turn out so well and succeed. So, in other words girl, if you arrest the prostitute on the street tonight, make sure you are polite to her the next time you meet."

When Dad concluded the terms of his conditions, he asked me, "Are you agreeable to these rules?"

I nodded my head and said, "Yes."

Dad then gave me one of his famous bear hugs, kissed me on the forehead and told me to go. Before I walked out of the door, I stopped in front of the statue of the Blessed Mother and kissed her on the head. As I genuflected in front of the icon of Mary, I said a silent prayer for her protection and guidance with this new-found career. I got up off of my knees and walked out of the door and down the stairs to the patrol car. The whole time I pondered on Dad's words. In that moment with the man that I respected most in the world, I was not quite clear of the significance of the words he had uttered. It would take me a few months in my new world of policing to fully comprehend the magnitude of his wisdom. It would take the arrest of a prostitute the first winter I worked. It would take a great deal of ribbing from my fellow male officers. It would take many hard knocks in those first eighteen months of policing. It would take the reconciliation of my heart and mind to fully comprehend his words and my resulting deeds as a compliance officer.

What I learned in the prevailing years of policing had to do with the importance of a legacy in fulfillment of one's life purpose. What we leave behind is our legacy to our families, friends and to the world. What my Father left behind was a true legacy and epitome of a good man, a devoted parent and a caring educator. Dad's love and kindness was reflected on his last day on this Earth as his family stood vigil when he took his last breaths. It was apparent at his funeral as innumerable people waited in line to view his body and tell us, his wife and children, of Dad's benevolence to them. Some of these people waited for hours to talk to us. These marvelous people took the time to come and share information. They told us about the times Dad bought them some food, a coat or a pair of shoes. They talked of the time he took to correct their ill behavior or give them accolades for an accomplishment. As each person talked they smiled and simultaneously shed a tear. Yes, this was the legacy of my Father to his wife, to his children, his family, his friends and this world. He had obviously fulfilled his destiny. He left his mark on this world in the very essence of all of his kind deeds. My father would often say that he "was not a perfect man and on any given day he would make mistakes."

However, on this day of remembrance of him, his mistakes were not apparent. For as the casket was closed inside the mausoleum at the cemetery, and as the trumpet played taps, all of the people present wept a river of tears and cried at his loss. As I looked across the room at all of the faces, I knew that my Dad had left his mark on this world. He had left his legacy of honor. Dad had done it in the name of God and humanity. This strong, handsome man, a mixture of kindness and gruffness had achieved his life's purpose. Dad had provided the opportunity for others to achieve excellence. I only hope when my days come to an end, I too have served my purpose and have allowed the opportunity for others to shine.

In these final moments of contemplation about this story of Flight 93 and the field of angels, I am sure a part of my legacy was in the telling of these events. It is my sacred contract in this lifetime to provide some information regarding a series of scenarios that culminated into this story.

It is also apparent that the families of the victims aboard Flight 93 can rest assured that their loved one's legacy was indeed left behind. It is a legacy of strength of character, bravery and love. It is a legacy to be told for many generations to come by their children and their children's children, who will hold their heads high in esteem in memory of their proud ancestry. May the passengers and crew members aboard Flight 93 rest in peace and know they left an unbelievable legacy of honor behind. All of us who live on through the ages will know these magnificent men and women provided for mankind and left their mark on humanity and on this world.

CHAPTER 26

A TALE OF TWO MUSES

A FEW YEARS AGO, A FRIEND WHO had traveled to Prague gave me a gift of six straw angels. He knew I collected them and thought I would enjoy these unique tiny dolls made exclusively of cornstalks. He believed they would enhance the angels that were already housed in the various locations of my home. These small and delicate figurines seemed to have a life of their own. They were tiny and fragile in appearance. Yet when held, they emitted great energy and warmth. On my first time holding them, I admired their beauty. As I sat by the river's edge looking at them, I was totally charmed. I instantly felt their energy. As I looked at the faces of these six tiny straw creatures, I heard a voice say,

"Give four away and keep two for yourself."

So, over the following year, I did just as I was requested to do. I gradually gave four of the angels to friends and acquaintances I encountered. Each of whom was having some difficulty in their life. As each of these people placed an angel in their hand, they commented on feeling an immediate warmth and energy swirling into their palms.

After having given the four angels away, I placed the two that I had kept for myself in my bedroom. I hung one on each side of my headboard. One of the angels held a book in its small hands and the other a set of cymbals. I was curious as to the choice of angels that I had coveted for my own safe keeping. Each of them resembled a facet of my life. A facet which not too many people knew existed in my personality. The book did so much depict a part of me who loved to read and write. I had written down my thoughts and feelings since I was sixteen years of age. The other equally displayed a hidden side of me. I loved music. It was a piece of me which my Mother had given to me. Her love of music had genetically passed on to me and some siblings. Even though she and I shared little with respect to our chosen paths, she had definitely provided me with this gene. I wasn't sure if my Mom was aware of this. But, I hoped in time she would be made aware and pleased with this knowledge.

As I lay in bed each night over the passing years, I could feel the angels' energy and I could hear their whispers in my ear. On one such night, I heard one of the angel's whisper,

"Get up and write."

So, I did as I was requested to do and over a period of three weeks I wrote the twenty odd chapters of my book.

A few days later, I heard the other whisper to me,

"Create a song."

So, once again I did as I was requested to do. As I stood in the shower that morning, I heard voices singing a song and violins playing in a rhythmic melody. The melodic rhapsody permeated my mind and body and pierced the very recesses of my soul. I then heard my own voice singing the words in tones of Gaelic tongue. The lyrics flowed as did the song. It was very slow paced and stirring. It lifted my mind to new levels and heights. I watched as my hands and arms were lifted and simulated the playing of the violin. I immediately wrote the words down on paper and captured the melody inside my head. To date, I have sung this song to several individuals and each responds in the same manner. The song stirs deep emotion in those that listen. In the past months, a young composer has brought the song to life. He has worked to complete a lovely composition of angelic design.

It wasn't until a few months following these events I realized what a wonderful gift I had received from my friend. He had not only given me the angels to add to my collection. He had given me a gift of two muses. These two lovely little angelic beings hanging on my headboard had opened up my mind. They had aided in the release of my higher power. They were indeed the muses of music and writing. The muse of writing as portrayed by the angel holding the book and the muse of music as depicted through the hands of the angel holding the cymbals. My muses had indeed stirred creativity in me and had channeled my God given hidden talents. I had previously written dating back to my teenage years. In fact in 1995, when I was home for an extended period of time following surgery, I even created a book of poetry entitled, "Thoughts of a Woman Named Trouble." The book was a compilation of poems I had written throughout my life. But in this long span of time, I had not constructively utilized this talent. It now appeared it was time to do so.

As I finished writing these last pages of my book, I took note of the special gifts in my life. I was deeply moved at the knowledge of how the pieces were all beginning to fit. These pieces were being strategically placed like a beautifully constructed mosaic. After all, life is a colorful mosaic of art as one piece fits with the other. Life is uniquely sculpted and crafted to create a finished product. If we get it right, we leave this Earth knowing we served our time well. Just like one's life, the selected pieces intertwine and segue to precision. One piece tightly fit and bound to the other. So, was my life. It emulated the paths so many others have taken before me. All patterned and intersected, weaving its path across time and space. Life is the many pieces of a puzzle all mixing to become the relevant points of passage in our life. All of these pieces are merged together to a final location and outcome. Our lives lead to our final destination and rebirth. I had been given my rebirth. Out of my pain and suffering, I had emerged triumphant and stronger. In the light of God, I have grown and become a better image to present in front of Him. I hope there is much more life yet ahead. I know there is much more I must strive to improve. However, life now seems so much sweeter and less bitter to the taste.

In the closing of this chapter, it appears I am able to turn a page in my life as well. I am grateful to my muses as they have moved me to reach for new horizons. To a life I had felt was unfulfilled prior to the writing of my book. In the writing of this book, I have accomplished a dream I set for myself almost forty years ago. I have found life does contain great happiness and joy. I have found my dream in the arms of my Father. He has provided me with an ending and a happier path to follow. If for some reason, I knew this was my last day on this Earth, I would leave knowing I have left my mark. I have left behind a lovely daughter who thrives and participates in this world.

She in turn has bore her children to grow and flourish among us. Like the fine-tuned story of others in our lives, I will leave behind my gift to humanity and I am ever hopeful I have done as God has asked.

CHAPTER 27

A CHRISTMAS SHAWL

A FEW DAYS PRIOR TO CHRISTMAS 2008, I received a package that bore the return address of a friend. My friend also happened to be a colleague that had served with me at the FBI. She and I had shared a genuine relationship that had flourished over the past few years. She had become one of my trusted compatriots and confidantes at work. We shared many a conversation and on occasion gifted each other with special intentions.

Our relationship was important to me because my friendships with my fellow employees was somewhat strained. Especially, those relationships with the older women in the office. These were the most difficult for me. From the onset of my employment, I was told there was a group of women who resented my hiring. Each of them had been interested in the job I had been appointed to do. Each had bid for it as part of the internal process of the Bureau. When none of them met the qualifications of the position, an external search for a qualified candidate was required. And, I was fortunate enough to be recruited and retained to fill the position as the Community Outreach Specialist.

However, the initial days of my employment primed me for what was yet to come. I was deemed the "outsider" and treated accordingly. On my third day at work, I received an unexpected welcoming from several of the women. I was in the stall of the office ladies room when I overheard three women talking about me. They were eagerly discussing their opinion of me and questioning my qualifications. Also, they made some innuendos as to whom they assumed I had slept with in order to get my job. Several names of men were suggested. I listened intently for a few minutes and then I exited the stall. By the look on their faces, they appeared shocked to see me. In as nonchalant a manner as possible, I strolled to the sink and soaped up my hands. I rinsed my hands in the warm water and tried to still my emotions and need to verbally lash out at them. I looked up into the mirror and saw each of their reflections was just staring in my direction. I politely smiled back at them. Their faces seemed to display feelings of disbelief at my ability to remain cordial. I turned off the facet and reached for some paper towels to dry off my hands. It was then I took the opportunity to speak. I said, "My qualifications for the position far exceed any of the other candidates who submitted an application. I have 14 years experience in law enforcement and six of those were in management. By all accounts, no other candidate could match my credentials, training and experience. And, if by chance each of you has slept your way to the top, don't base your behavior on mine. I don't play where I work."

As I turned to walk away, I added one last comment. "By the way, based on this incident, each of you has chosen the wrong profession. You don't belong in law enforcement. In my experience, I would have made sure the person I was gossiping about was not present in the room. Next time, check the stall before you open your mouths."

I walked out of the door and made a bee-line straight to my Boss's office. Once there, I unloaded on him and told him about the incident in the ladies room. He listened intently and allowed me to finish. When I was done speaking, he said, "What am I chopped liver? How come I'm not on that list of men you have slept with?"

At first, I looked at him in disbelief. He then added, "I was trying to add some levity to the situation. Are you alright? Do you want me to talk with the women?"

I replied, "I'm fine and no I don't need anyone to fight my battles. Especially you. They'll just add you to the list of suspected lovers."

I left his office wondering what had I done. When I made the decision to accept the Bureau's offer of employment, I thought there would be a higher standard of behavior. After all, the Bureau had always represented itself as the premier law enforcement agency in the Country. But in my mind, those initial days in the Bureau had indicated otherwise. By all accounts, it seemed to operate on the same level as the other agencies I had worked for. It left me wondering about my choice.

In the past, my relationships with other women were strained, but it was generally related to my position as a police officer. In the early stages of my law enforcement career, not many women chose it as a profession. So, for the most part, I had very little in common with other females. Even the older women in my family had a tough time comprehending why I would want to be a cop. And when I began working at the police department, the officer's wives often expressed their resentment regarding my working relationship with their husbands. This was the first of the difficulties I experienced, but one I tried to comprehend and resolve. Over time, many of the wives came to change their opinions and became more comfortable with me. Some of them even became a friend.

After the incident in the ladies room, it took me some time before someone in the office enlightened me on the subject. One of the women who had resented my hiring was eager to explain the reasons behind her ill feelings and those of the other women. She explained it had much to do regarding the past precedent of promotions in the Bureau. It seemed from the earliest history of the Bureau, promotions were handled only from within. Many of those promoted achieved the status because of their longevity of employment and not any specialized skills. But with the present administration at FBI Headquarters (FBIHQ), a new hiring practice had begun. All candidates for any jobs posted were required to meet a new standard of hiring. In order to apply (both internally and externally) those being considered had to meet the education, training, practical experience, knowledge, skills and abilities of the job requirements. This new hiring practice had caused a great stir within the Bureau. Hence, with no ability to argue their points of contention with the policy makers at FBIHQ, all of the ill feelings seemed to be directed at me. This woman went on to elaborate there was additional resentment because of my entry grade level and base pay. She also couldn't wait to relate she and others in the office had bestowed the nickname of "slagent" when referring to me. It was a name given to describe my position. It seemed there were many questions as to what my duties and responsibilities included. When described to any interested party, I was placed in this new category of employees who had job descriptions which were both support and agent in nature. I was branded with the new title and wasn't quite sure as to how to respond to it. Over the years to come, it was a nickname used by some of the employees in the office. And I was never quite sure when it was used to be vindictive or complimentary.

So on the day I received the package, I hesitated to open it. I had not heard from my friend for a few months. She had not even made one telephone call to inquire about the state of my health. Her lack of interest in my well-being had hurt my feelings. Prior to this day, I had thought of her quite often. I had even made two telephone calls to the office in hopes of hearing her voice on the other end of the phone. It had only been a couple of days prior I had lamented this very issue to a family member. I had related I was upset because I had not heard from my friend. I had believed that she of all people would have taken a few moments out of her busy day to contact me. I was very disappointed in her apparent lack of concern.

With the arrival of the package, my mood changed. I was elated to see her name on it. I opened the package a little weary of the contents. To my surprise, I found a lovely prayer shawl contained inside the plain brown box. The shawl bore the colors of pale blue, green, lavender and a smidgen of ivory. It was soft to the touch and intricately woven in design. As I unwrapped the beautiful piece of woven wool, I found a note from my friend. On it she had written some kind words and wishes for a speedy recovery. Also, her note explained that the shawl had been knitted by her and other church members at her congregation. It had been knitted while they all prayed for me. As I read the note, my eyes filled with tears for her kindness and her gift. I felt so relieved to know someone truly cared about me and my safe return to health. I held the shawl close to my heart and said a prayer for the Blessing of my friend and for her honorable intentions on my behalf.

A few nights later, I wasn't feeling very well. I had been suffering with a great deal of pain in my neck, arms and hands. The tingling sensation in my right hand was causing some real discomfort for me. As I prepared to go to bed, I had the occasion to place the shawl around my shoulders. As I swirled the shawl around the upper part of my body, I immediately felt heat in the middle of my back. The warmest sensation began running across my back to my shoulders and down both of my arms. I felt a deep sense of comfort. It was as if I could feel the energy contained inside the shawl magically intertwine with mine. It seemed that each of the interlocking weaves resembled a prayer said on my behalf. I could hear the whispers of each woman's voice that had invoked God to help me heal. I could almost see the women in their picturesque setting of the church as they knitted and shared pleasantries with each other. I could feel each finger as it delicately placed the yarn around the needle and pulled a stitch in place. As I ran my hand down the multi-colored softly woven tapestry, my mind relaxed and opened to the positive concept of healing. And, within a few moments of time, I fell asleep on my bed.

As I slept, I dreamt of the field and its angels. I was carried back to the scene of arrival at the Flight 93 crash site. I saw the line of angels surrounding the vehicle. I saw the darkness around the angels as it lay there densely against the ground. All at once, the dark areas on the ground turned to a bright red coloration and started to swirl in a violent pattern of movement. The red coloration twisted into a tightly bound cylinder similar to the shape of a tornado. All at once, I saw a shape taking form. The form then became clearer and it morphed into that of my impression of a demon. I saw the evil face with its deep soul-less eyes. I saw the terrible features of torment all displayed upon its face. The form twisted in great fury and gave a mighty roar.

With its mouth gaped open, it then moved in a swift pattern across the ground. I felt the sensation of its breath upon my brow. My ears rang with the loudness of its voice. I awoke in great fear of my safety. I called out to Archangel Michael for his help.

As I yelled out Michael's name, I saw the image of Jesus rising from His tomb. He was draped in a loosely-fit white garb that flowed as He moved across the ground. His arm was raised to the sky and He was carrying a banner that bore a cross on it. As Jesus moved toward the direction of the demon, He stopped and stood directly above him. Jesus said nothing but merely stayed in His place awaiting the next move. This next move came in the beckoning of His angels.

I saw a shimmer of pale pink light appear and begin to take form. The pink formation moved and began to grow and expand in its size. As a set of wings appeared, I heard the words, "Ariel has arrived."

Ariel did appear and took her position behind Jesus as did Michael and the rest of the angels. They all moved in line behind her. Ariel began to move in the direction of the devil and she swirled her lovely hued form straight toward him. As the two forms clashed, I again heard words being spoken. "It is the final battle of good and evil. On this sacred ground, all that is good will conquer all that is evil. In this place, it will be done."

As these words are uttered, I saw the most amazing burst of light. As the light faded, I saw that the image of the demon was gone. All that was left in the place where he once stood lay the softest of white lights across the formerly darkened ground.

When I awoke from this dream, I couldn't help but wonder as to the true meaning of the events that took place. I understood the importance of the battle between good and evil in the depiction of the forms moving from the darkness into the light. I also truly believed that this battle was a necessary part of the events at the crash site. In the first moments of seeing the demon rising from the red coloration, I was terrified at its depiction. I had awakened to hear myself calling to Michael. He swiftly responded to my cries for help and brought with him the lovely Ariel. As I remembered the warm sensation of my protector's arrival, I also recalled Ariel is also an Archangel. She is the Archangel of strength and courage. Ariel is the angel who is called upon in a time of need to draw one's strength to respond. Her likeness is often depicted as a lioness. On this night of my descent into the path of evil, she roared at the formations of the night and drove them back into their dark domain.

I found myself asking what else was depicted by the presence of this dark domain. I knew there was a hidden meaning I had not yet grasped. For dreams do often contain the answers to my questions. As I spent time contemplating the underlying meaning of this dream, I became keenly aware the devil symbolized my fear of the personal demon I have been struggling with. The fury of the demon depicted the wrath I was feeling inside. I was angry at myself for failing. By becoming ill, I had failed those I loved, those I served and myself in some obscure way. As human beings we struggle with the good and evil in ourselves and others. Like those others, my life has been represented by the image of an angel on one shoulder telling me to do good and the demon on the other shoulder telling me to be malicious. It was in this moment of ponder I realized the demon was indeed symbolic of the fears which menaced my body and mind. I had fallen into a great abyss of anxiety and had buried myself in the deep dark hole. Just like the battle depicted on the field, I had been engaged in a struggle as well.

The next morning, I awoke to find the shawl still tightly wrapped around me. As I sat up in the bed, I noticed the pain was gone. For ten days, I had suffered with the tightness in my neck and back and the tingling in my arms and hands. All had dissipated during the night. During this Christmas season, I had been fortunate to receive yet another gift to enhance my already Blessed life. I was gifted with this delicately woven prayer shawl. The shawl had been sent to aid me in my healing by someone who I knew also shared my belief in God and His mercy. I hoped that someday I would be able to return her kindness and provide her with a Christmas present of equal magnitude. In the meantime, I would say a silent prayer for her safe keeping.

CHAPTER 28

THE RETURN OF AN
OLD PATTERN

SHORTLY AFTER THE BEGINNING OF THE NEW YEAR, I returned to my weekly scheduled visits with the psychologist. Over the Christmas Holiday, I had time to reflect about the entire story that had unfolded during the therapy sessions. It was a story that could only be digested in the re-reading of the events. I am still astounded each time I look at the story's pages that reflect the messages from the Most Blessed Mother as she defines the need for all of us to change. As part of my weekly sessions, the psychologist incorporated a second type of therapy. This therapy was called "heart math" and was used for purposes of getting the electronics of the heart healthier. The name heart math did not resonate well with me at first. I had a tough time believing that my heart could be synchronized in a pattern that would not react to the anxiety. As I thought about it sitting in the all too familiar chair and office, I knew that I was once again witnessing the reemergence of my ego. It was the same ego that I had wrestled with for so long. I thought that it had disappeared in my final recognition of the PTSD diagnosis and the exit of my "superwoman" persona. Unfortunately, my ego hadn't gone away. It merely lay in waiting for the right opportunity to pounce again and take control.

On February 3, 2009, as I sat describing for the psychologist my feelings and my disappointment in my inability to move forward in my healing, I told her I felt there was still a part of my brain that was congested. I explained I could feel the blockage in the left lower side of my head and of the headaches that plagued me on a routine basis. When I had finished expressing my concern, we discussed my thoughts on what was causing the congestion to remain. It was a question I had no answer for. With my reply, the psychologist began the EMDR session. She asked me the routine introductory questions and I placed myself once again on the hill above the beaches of Southwestern Ireland.

In seconds, my mind opened up to a new scene I had not viewed before. I could see the inner spaces of my brain with all of its grey matter twisted in miraculous weaved turns. As my eyes traveled across the narrow passages of my brain, I became transfixed on a red coloration at the left base area. This section appeared to be inflamed and pulsing at a much quicker level than the other areas of my mind. It looked raw and angry in its form. As I tried to look closer at the reddened area of my brain, my eyes shifted and I again traveled to the vision of the angels on the desolate field. I could hear the angels whispering to me that the lower corridor of my brain still burns red. It is red with flames for the leftover feelings of regret and my inability to forgive myself. I can not pardon myself for the feelings which momentarily incapacitated me at the site. I can not accept the fear within me. In the lower left area of my mind, I had sustained the inadequate feeling of powerlessness. I believed what I had sensed was something negative was about to happen. The sensation I had was one of foreboding and similar to those I felt so many years ago as I patrolled the streets as a police officer. Buried in the redness that remained inextinguishable in the dark areas of my mind, I felt guilty for my inability to prevent the events of 9-11. I too had anger toward the egos of the organization that I had served.

As I viewed the red shadowed area of my mind, I heard Michael's words once again spoken. This time his words were intended for me. He said, "Move forward in God's design. Quit holding on out of fear and the lack of redemption for yourself. Place yourself back into the hands of God. The Blessings and gifts must be used and not hidden. The people in your life for the next three months are here to guide and protect you. The self protection you seek is not necessary. The hand of God touches you and provides you with an opening to the gateway. You must practice your craft on a daily basis. I promise you all will make sense and all will be true. The manuscript flies over New York for three more weeks. Keep the faith as the rest of the channels open. Those that came before you are also protecting you and I never leave. In God's name, I say to you let go. Your path lies before you now."

A lovely and vibrant cobalt blue light flashes in front of my mind's eye. I feel peaceful and my mind has calmed. It has been quieted by the effect of Michael's words and their meaning. I am enlightened by the message from Michael as he reiterates to me that I am bound to the interconnectedness of us all. It is an all encompassing message that passes through the soul and reverberates its meaning to the mind. I still awaken in the darkness on many nights and revel in the knowledge of their meanings. How exquisite was the language used in its purity of content. In the stillness of the night the words and their meanings resonate to the deepest parts of my soul. As each is contemplated, the vastness in its approach to bring a new order for all humanity to intertwine into one is a marvel to bestow.

And, in the luxury of each moment I languish in the wonder of the defined meaning and the principles that they bear for us all.

CHAPTER 29

LOOKING FOR A PIECE
OF MYSELF

FOR ALL TOO MANY YEARS NOW, I have asked myself: why does the field at Shanksville not leave my mind's eye? It stays pictured in the stillness of the film that repeatedly rewinds and plays back time and time again. With each rewind of the tape, I stay stuck and fixated on the vision of me, standing there just looking out over the expanse of the ground. Although the scene has changed in its reflection, my mind still can not move past this domain.

The trees no longer hold the horrific details staring down upon my brow. There are no more smells of burning pine trees or fumes of jet fuel irritating and lingering in the nostrils of my nose. No more remnants of lives lost or things left undone. No more stolen moments of what could have been and no last words to be said as the bagpiper plays the final note of his sullen melody. The field has taken on a different version than before. Now, each time it is displayed across the frames of my mind, I see myself standing there just looking across the terrain.

As I stare into the distant place of the "field of glory", my mind wonders to some deep abyss where caverns of secret places unfold before me. I wonder why I continue to stare at what is not there. Had I missed some detail all of those years ago? Was there some task yet to do? Or, was I still grieving the loss of life or the insanity of the deed? The answers to these questions came quite by surprise one warm September evening as I sat talking with a dear friend. As we spoke about life, the events of 9-11, the past years of ill health and my inability to heal and move forward from the place on the field, he provided me with a profound insight that had not occurred to me before. "You keep looking to find yourself. You left some part of you on that field all those years ago and you keep waiting for her to return. She's out there. You just have to bring her back home."

When he finished speaking, I was flooded with a feeling of emotion. It all began to make sense to me. I questioned whether his thoughts held the answer to my healing. Had I left so much of me behind on the field that there was no ability to move forward into a present life? As soon as he had uttered these words, something clicked inside my head and the connection of the relativity of his statement rang clear. He was absolutely right. I had lost myself on that day of September 11th, 2001. The woman I knew for all of my years had drifted away from me and had not yet returned. She had turned into a person who somehow always seemed to be in a "battle mode." Gone was the true essence of me. I had become this vigilant warrior always watching and anxious for the bad tidings to come. The soft creature of my youth had gone by and lay stranded on the field. It was as if I had been kidnapped and held unwillingly in some abode of an unknown location.

As we sat there and spoke, I realized this man fully understood my feelings. He "got me" and my thoughts. He was speaking from his own experiences in life. He had served a tour of duty during the Vietnam War and he had once told me he never came back home the same person. He always felt he was never quite right again. He understood all too well the "hauntings" and the sullen moods which crept up for no apparent reason but that of a memory sustained. He was just an 18 year old kid traveling to a place far from home, from the comfort of his family and his friends, and arriving in an unfamiliar destination were he saw things no human being should ever witness in their lives.

He had left a young man. With hopes and dreams which were filled with such promise of happiness. He came home a man. No longer allowed any feelings to surrender to the true essence of his heart. He was frozen in those moments of his memory about a life he left thousands of miles away.

To this day, when he speaks I can still see a far away look in his eyes. It tells me he has once again traveled back to the place where he left his heart and a piece of his sanity so long ago. In a shared moment on my front porch that evening, I heard his heart beckon to me in full understanding of what we both experienced. It was a place beset by memories of pain and sadness. It was a past dwelling where we had each left behind a piece of ourselves.

Now, in the quiet stillness of this full moonlit night, came the knowledge of an answer so long sought. With this newfound revelation, it was apparent all I needed to do was make the choice to return. I became determined when the next flashback of the field entered my mind, I simply needed to visualize myself turning around and walking away. I needed to say my "goodbyes" and just walk back into this current life and my present reality. It was a solution which seemed to hold such promise for my recovery. I only hoped with this newfound knowledge, my friend would take his own advice and finally walk back into his life as well. I only hoped somewhere inside him lay his answers and maybe I could help him recover the soldier he too had left behind on his battlefield of long ago.

BATTLE PRONE

MY MIND IS CONSTANTLY BESIEGED WITH THE thoughts of my next battle. It is unwavering in its design. It stands fast and ready as it awaits the next enemy to move across the horizon of my mind's refrain. I am battle prone in my stance. Who might it be, I hear in my ears? I feel it in my body as the tension presses in on me. I see myself as the ever-vigilant warrior awaiting a foe who will allow me no quarter and no rest. The next round of destruction and pain is clearly stated upon the recesses of my mind. I await an outcome with my pulse surging and my eyes intent on their next movement. If I waver, they may arrive unnoticed. If a reprisal is necessary, I must be prepared to strike back swiftly and with no mercy. The battle readiness remains a perpetual part of my being. As one deluge passes, the other prepares to leap inside and take hold of the darkest parts of my brain. When will I just be at peace again? When will the fear, anxiety and the anger leave my tired brow? I stand isolated on this lonely field of glory just waiting for the next gladiator to appear.

CHAPTER 30

EMDR THERAPY

IN JUNE OF 2008, MY JOURNEY TO healing took another turn in the road. After months and months of conventional therapy, I was frustrated over my inability to make any headway and move forward to a place of healing. It appeared that I was stalemated by the anxiety and continued re-occurrences of the memories of the field. At this time in my life, I was desperate for any possible relief from the flashbacks, the emotional and physical pain. It just so happened that during a conversation with a man who was once my boss at the FBI, there was something of a breakthrough for me. It was during this very talk I first heard of a possible therapy that may help me in my recovery. This man was someone I had grown to respect. Since his retirement from the Bureau, he had become a close friend and confidante. During our discussion, I told him about my concerns that my current therapy sessions didn't seem to be helping me. On the contrary, I explained, it felt more like I was spinning in a motion of circles and sinking deeper into the thick murk of the memories with no real ability to clear the way to recovery. As we spoke, he suggested I discuss with my psychologist the option of a therapy known as Eye Movement Desensitization Reprocessing (EMDR).

As we continued to talk, he further explained what EMDR was and that it had been used for many years to aid military personnel and law enforcement officers after they had been exposed to some traumatic event while serving in the line of duty. He was then kind enough to share with me a personal story. He too had been deeply affected by an incident when he had served as a supervisory agent in Puerto Rico. He told me about how he had learned about EMDR and had undergone the treatment following an undercover investigation that had left one of his colleagues murdered. As he described in vivid detail the events which led up to his involvement in the investigation, the shooting, the funeral and his ultimate decision to engage in EMDR, my mind connected with his thought process and I felt the need to pursue the option of his suggestion.

When he was finished with his story about the traumatic events that led to the critical injury of his comrade, I found myself crying and I could hear the emotion in his voice too. Despite the years that had separated the actual event, he was still deeply touched by the memory of his fallen colleague and I found myself affected by the loss as well. My heart ached for him as it did hearing about the poor man who had lost his life while serving. However, my tears were shed for a twofold reason. I was tearful for the loss but, equally relieved to know yet another strong and capable man whom I admired had openly admitted that at a time in his life, during a highly successful career, he too had needed help to restore his life. I can't describe the feeling of relief to know that someone understood how I felt. For too long, the sense of isolation had taken over me and my need to distance myself from others at times became so pronounced. To hear the revelation of another, and most especially a man, as he confessed his pain and deep hurt following an event, greatly reassured me I was not alone in my knowledge of the dark abyss which my mind had somehow fallen into.

The revelation of his sharing seemed to cause my intuition to stir and I wanted to learn more about the EMDR. Despite my consistency in attending the weekly sessions, I had made no real progress or gained any relief to my fractured psyche. My mind still traveled to the Shanksville field and reminded me of all of the sights and sounds of the prevailing days at the crash site. All of the therapy did not prevent these elements from being a constant reminder of the event. I had tired of the constant "hauntings" as my mind traveled to the site time and time again. It had gotten so painful to relive and I feared the nights most when I had to shut my eyes and dream. Each night when I saw the field, and each morning when I woke, it was still there before my eyes. So when my friend had mentioned EMDR, I was ready to grab at any suggested remedy which might aid my healing.

A few days following our talk, it was once again time for my weekly visit to the therapist. After going through the routine checklist about my current health status that included those two questions I resented most (about suicidal or homicidal thoughts), I asked her what she knew about EMDR. She explained to me that EMDR was a powerful method of psychotherapy. It was used to help relieve many types of psychological distress. During a session, the therapist works with the patient to identify a specific problem as the focus of the treatment session. The patient is then requested to recall disturbing memories which were seen, heard or felt. The therapist uses the movement of their fingers to stimulate the brain while the patient focuses on the disturbing event. As part of the EMDR, the patient may experience intense emotions that have lain dormant for too long. Sometimes, the memory will recall additional information that caused the initial traumatic effect to the patient. The therapist then concluded her thoughts by saying that she felt EMDR was a good option for me to consider. She added, although the therapy would force me to remember the events of 9-11, it may help bring relief to the sharp images, smells and sounds that had caused the traumatic effects to my psyche. In turn, it may begin the process to relieve my pain and heal some of the chronic health problems.

As we finished our discussion, I asked if she would contact my primary care physician and the psychologist at the FBI to determine if the EMDR therapy was a good choice for me and if so, was there a doctor who could be recommended to pursue treatment. It took a few more weeks of back and forth dialogue between the two to locate a doctor in Pittsburgh who included EMDR as part of the practice. In July of 2008, a psychologist was identified and I attended my first therapy session. My initial visit with the psychologist was one filled with great anxiety and hesitation. However, as I worked with the new psychologist, I began to embrace the idea of opening my mind to the possibility of healing. If EMDR was the proven method of treatment, then I had little choice in the matter. Regardless of any hesitation on my part, it was now time to dig into the dark corners of my mind and relive the events which had caused so much trauma and wreaked havoc to my life. It was now time to deal directly with the ghosts who had haunted and had immobilized me with fear. If I was to truly heal, I was going to have to place my trust in this psychologist and in her abilities to help open my mind as a means of releasing the pain. I only hoped I would grow to trust her as she helped me through the process. To my surprise, the EMDR sessions did bring about the remembering of the traumatic events of 9-11, but more importantly helped in the expansion of my spirituality and a deeper understanding of my faith and my religious beliefs. The resulting factor was my mind's ability to open to the intuitive gifts we all have. It seemed mine had been blocked by all of the memories of the field. I only hoped in time there would be some additional clarity as my mind began to clear the sludge from its clogged passageways.

CHAPTER 31

A SYMBOL OF RESURRECTION

WHEN THE AIRPLANES HIT THE THREE DESTINATIONS of the Twin Towers, the Pentagon and the Shanksville landfill, the indescribable destruction that was left in their wake still remains a part of our daily lives in America. To this day, the aftermath of death, injury and the lasting pain of the survivors has been a part of our society since the planes flew across the summer skies on September 11th. The once confident stride of America was bruised and our trust in others was breached. Ten years later, remnants of that devasation still remain, challenging our country's economy and many others as well.

However, out of the ashes of the ruins at each of these three sites, rose symbols of our faith that reminded us that God was here that September day.

As the mighty towers crashed to the streets in New York, a symbolic gesture of God stood erect in the abstraction of a large metal cross. It was a cross that was not man made but self designed when the metal girders of the building finally settled at the base of ground zero. To all that looked at it on a daily basis, it brought hope for life sustained and of a possible future of reconciliation to all.

Additionally, there has been many a story written by Ground Zero responders, survivors and family members of the Twin Tower's victims who attest to visions of their deceased loved ones and colleagues. Each person who has spoken of such visits from the beyond are convinced the visions were real. Each individual described the warm and loving feeling emitted by their visitor. And, they explained how the apparition brought a sense of peace and comfort to them during their time of grief.

As the Pentagon burned, there were all too many reminders of the damage left behind and the carnage apparent at every turn taken in the building designed to defend. But, out of the downed structure, some limestone was saved and four crosses were designed and made from the ruins. The crosses were created to symbolize death, rebirth and new life. A cross was then gifted to all of the three crash sites. At the time of my medical leave, the cross gifted to the Pittsburgh Field Office stood in the corner of my office. It had been placed there by the man who had designed it. Other than being exhibited for a short period of time in a local historical museum, my office had been its home since the onset of its arrival in Pittsburgh.

At the Shanksville landfill, God set the gift of a field of angels to remind us of His ever sustaining love. Out of the dark soot of the damaged landfill, the angels and the souls of the faithfully departed rose and moved to God's light. This is my testimony of faith, hope and love. And, it is a testament of the higher power that was not only seen by me, but by others who have sensed its presence when they stand and walk on the hallowed ground of the field.

At each of these sites, there was recognition of God's omnipresence. He was present for those who died, for those who suffered, for those who bore witness, for those who responded and gave aid, and for those who were raised to a level of heroism. Each person who played a role in this unfathomable event felt God and His everlasting grace. It gave credence to the saying, "Bravery is only great when there is no hope." In those first few moments of the horrendous events, there seemed little to be hopeful of. Yet, as has been the case throughout our religious history, in our darkest times, God has sent us all signs to bear witness of His kindness toward mankind.

Although the cross signifies great suffering to many of us based upon our religious beliefs, it is also symbolic of God's promise for resurrection. And, in the fallen times of our country's history, the cross has been used as a sign of great hope to those who believe in life after death. In humanity's moment of extreme strife, humiliation and the pain of 9-11, this symbol of inspiration arose from the black holes of sorrow in our Earthly hell that day. The light was sent to help illuminate our lives to our recovery. Those who doubted God's presence on that fateful day were provided a sign of His deep love for us and His hope for our redemption. God gave us the message of the cross to remind us of His amazing grace and His belief in humanity's ability to prevail. On that day, there were signs of hope. It was a hope of survival and a reminder we are all designed in the image of our Creator and each responsible one to the other.

EPILOGUE

SOMEDAY, IN THE DISTANT FUTURE OF TIME and space, long after the generations which survived the events of 9-11 are gone from their Earthly domain, a small star will appear and shoot across the horizon. The star will travel and shine down upon the field at Shanksville. As it shimmers in the night sky, children will look at it in wonder. Just like the storytellers from medieval times, these children's parents will "tell the tale" of the field of angels and the heroes of Flight 93. As the star twinkles in the darkness of the universe's indigo abyss, it will be a reminder of the great deed done. A deed completed to fulfill life's purpose. The purpose of many lives that moved all too swiftly from birth to death to rebirth. When this tiny star of light shoots across the vastness of the sky, so will the memories of these events lie limitless in the mind's design. For courage and valor are the best of human traits displayed and these values were shared by those that perished on the plane.

AUTHOR'S CLOSING NOTE

AS THIS BOOK CLOSES ITS CHAPTERS, I want to make sure to clarify an issue or two. If for some reason the contents of the book left you wondering why it did not provide more in-depth information about the FBI, please understand it is because of Bureau policy. In order to publish a book, a current or former employee must abide by the policies which are mandated by the Bureau. Any publication may not contain any information which may be perceived as either "classified" or "sensitive" in nature. In order to meet the standard of this doctrine, I have drafted the information contained in this book in a generic form. So, if I have left the reader with questions yet unanswered, I apologize, but ask you understand the constraints of my former employment.

The opinions expressed in these chapters are those of Lillie Leonardi and not of the FBI.

ABOUT THE AUTHOR

LILLIE AND HER DAUGHTER

AFTER SERVING FOR 25 YEARS AND AS a result of medical issues related to her Post Traumatic Stress Disorder (PTSD) diagnosis, Lillie retired from the law enforcement profession and now endeavors to pursue her lifetime passion for writing.

From 1998 to 2010, Lillie Leonardi was employed by the Federal Bureau of Investigation (FBI), Pittsburgh Division, as its Community Affairs Coordinator. During her tenure with the FBI, Lillie's primary focus and research related to the topic of violence prevention. She also worked under the auspice of the United States Attorney's Office, Western District of Pennsylvania and served with a prestigious group of instructors who provided training on various subjects including: Community Policing, Crime Prevention, Cultural Diversity, Hate Crimes, Responding to a Major Incident, Threat Assessment and Violence Reduction Techniques, as well as other related topics.

Immediately following the crash of Flight 93 in Shanksville, Pennsylvania; Lillie was deployed to the site where she spent the next 13 days. During that time, she was tasked to serve as the primary liaison to the United Airlines humanitarian response team, officials from the Japanese Government, as well as other law enforcement, government and social service entities and assisted in the coordination of the two memorial services.

Post 9-11, Lillie was utilized by the FBI as the contact for three other projects relating to Flight 93. She was a consulting representative with the Smithsonian Institute in Washington, DC; the Senator John Heinz History Museum located in Pittsburgh, Pennsylvania; as well as the Flight 93 Oral History Project coordinated by the Department of Interior and based in Somerset, Pennsylvania.

Prior to her career with the FBI, Lillie worked as the lead law enforcement officer on two college campuses located in Pittsburgh, Pennsylvania. She was appointed the first female Chief of Police for Chatham University (1994) and the Director of Security for Carlow University (1992). In 1984, Lillie was appointed to serve as the first female police officer with the City of Arnold, Pennsylvania. While employed with the police department, she specialized in crimes against children investigations and crime prevention.

National Park Foundation

"A portion of the proceeds from the sale of this book will be donated to the National Park Foundation to aid in the construction of the Flight 93 National Memorial. To make a tax-deductible donation to support the Memorial go to www.honorflight93.org/donate."

(The Flight 93 National Memorial is a project of the National Park Foundation. The Foundation is the non-profit charitable partner of the America's national parks.)

WA